The examination of witnesses in court : including examination in chief, cross-examination, and re-examination.

Frederic John Wrottesley

The examination of witnesses in court : including examination in chief, cross-examination, and re-examination.
Wrottesley, Frederic John
collection ID CTRG97-B1345
Reproduction from York University Law School Library
Includes indexes.
London : Sweet & Maxwell, 1910.
iv, 178 p. : forms ; 23 cm

The Making of Modern Law collection of legal archives constitutes a genuine revolution in historical legal research because it opens up a wealth of rare and previously inaccessible sources in legal, constitutional, administrative, political, cultural, intellectual, and social history. This unique collection consists of three extensive archives that provide insight into more than 300 years of American and British history. These collections include:

Legal Treatises, 1800-1926: over 20,000 legal treatises provide a comprehensive collection in legal history, business and economics, politics and government.

Trials, 1600-1926: nearly 10,000 titles reveal the drama of famous, infamous, and obscure courtroom cases in America and the British Empire across three centuries.

Primary Sources, 1620-1926: includes reports, statutes and regulations in American history, including early state codes, municipal ordinances, constitutional conventions and compilations, and law dictionaries.

These archives provide a unique research tool for tracking the development of our modern legal system and how it has affected our culture, government, business – nearly every aspect of our everyday life. For the first time, these high-quality digital scans of original works are available via print-on-demand, making them readily accessible to libraries, students, independent scholars, and readers of all ages.

old books, new life.

The BiblioLife Network

This project was made possible in part by the BiblioLife Network (BLN), a project aimed at addressing some of the huge challenges facing book preservationists around the world. The BLN includes libraries, library networks, archives, subject matter experts, online communities and library service providers. We believe every book ever published should be available as a high-quality print reproduction; printed on-demand anywhere in the world. This insures the ongoing accessibility of the content and helps generate sustainable revenue for the libraries and organizations that work to preserve these important materials.

The following book is in the "public domain" and represents an authentic reproduction of the text as printed by the original publisher. While we have attempted to accurately maintain the integrity of the original work, there are sometimes problems with the original work or the micro-film from which the books were digitized. This can result in minor errors in reproduction. Possible imperfections include missing and blurred pages, poor pictures, markings and other reproduction issues beyond our control. Because this work is culturally important, we have made it available as part of our commitment to protecting, preserving, and promoting the world's literature.

GUIDE TO FOLD-OUTS MAPS and OVERSIZED IMAGES

The book you are reading was digitized from microfilm captured over the past thirty to forty years. Years after the creation of the original microfilm, the book was converted to digital files and made available in an online database.

In an online database, page images do not need to conform to the size restrictions found in a printed book. When converting these images back into a printed bound book, the page sizes are standardized in ways that maintain the detail of the original. For large images, such as fold-out maps, the original page image is split into two or more pages

Guidelines used to determine how to split the page image follows:

• Some images are split vertically; large images require vertical and horizontal splits.
• For horizontal splits, the content is split left to right.
• For vertical splits, the content is split from top to bottom.
• For both vertical and horizontal splits, the image is processed from top left to bottom right.

THE EXAMINATION OF WITNESSES IN COURT

INCLUDING

EXAMINATION IN CHIEF, CROSS-EXAMINATION, AND RE-EXAMINATION

FOUNDED ON

"The Art of Winning Cases," by Henry Hardwicke, of the New York Bar,

AND

"The Advocate," by Edward W. Cox, Serjeant-at-Law

ADAPTED FOR THE USE OF ENGLISH READERS
AND REVISED UP TO DATE

BY

FREDERIC JOHN WROTTESLEY

OF THE INNER TEMPLE, BARRISTER-AT-LAW

LONDON
SWEET & MAXWELL, Ltd.
3 CHANCERY LANE

TORONTO
THE CARSWELL CO., Ltd.
19 DUNCAN STREET

1910

PREFACE.

WHEN I was asked by Messrs. Sweet and Maxwell to adapt that part of Mr. Hardwicke's book which deals with the examination of witnesses, for English readers, my first intention was merely to annotate those passages which, owing to the difference between the practice of the two countries, seemed to require it.

But on attempting to do this, I found that, in respect of discovery and other interlocutory matters, the differences of procedure, though slight in principle, were so numerous as to make the result unwieldy. Consequently I abandoned the attempt, and substituted the first chapter of the present book, which gives the beginner a rough sketch of the manner in which evidence documentary and otherwise, is obtained from opponents before the trial.

Similarly with regard to the chapters on the treatment of witnesses in Court, I have been obliged from time to time to take liberties with the text of Mr. Hardwicke's work. So far as questions of policy and rules of conduct for the advocate are concerned, I have left the text practically untouched. And Mr. Cox's book, from which Mr. Hardwicke borrowed largely, was written for advocates practising in the English Courts

But in matters relating to professional etiquette, the separation of the two professions of barrister and solicitor in England has made it necessary to alter or re-write passages which Mr. Hardwicke wrote for the combined profession. And in matters which depend upon the law of evidence strictly regarded, the increasing scope of codifying statutes, such as the Criminal Evidence Act, 1898, made it more convenient to re-write those passages which are affected by these statutes.

Finally, I have added a chapter on some elementary rules of evidence, in the belief that a list of such rules, especially if it be short, may be of use to the beginner in advocacy.

F. J. WROTTESLEY.

6, PUMP COURT,
TEMPLE,
July, 1910

TABLE OF CONTENTS.

———◆———

TABLE OF CASES CITED

THE EXAMINATION OF WITNESSES.

CHAPTER I.

PRELIMINARY STEPS.

IT was a maxim of the Common Law that "no man is bound to arm an adversary against himself." But the effect of this maxim has been very largely discounted by the modern provisions for Discovery. And the success or failure of the advocate in examining and cross-examining the parties and witnesses at the trial depends so often on the judicious use of these provisions for Discovery, that a short sketch of the manner in which they should be employed has been given.

Documentary evidence, in the shape of correspondence, or otherwise, forms an ever-increasing and ever more important part of the evidence in all kinds of actions. And at the commencement of an action a litigant and his advisers generally find that several documents, which are material to his case, are in the possession of his opponent. It is, therefore, vital that he should have an opportunity of inspecting these documents and of taking copies of them, where necessary.

The means of doing this are provided by the Rules of the Supreme Court, and especially by Order XXXI.

Order XXXI., Rule 12, provides that :—

Any party may, without filing any affidavit, apply to the Court or Judge for an order directing any other party to any cause or matter to make discovery on oath of the documents which are or have been in his possession or power, relating to any matter in question therein. On the hearing of such application the Court or Judge may either refuse or adjourn the same, if satisfied that such discovery is not necessary, or not necessary at that stage of the cause or matter, or make such order, either generally or limited to certain classes of documents, as may in their or his discretion be thought fit. Provided that discovery shall not be ordered when and so far as the Court or Judge shall be of opinion that it is not necessary either for disposing fairly of the cause or matter or for saving costs.

Generally speaking, in the K. B D., the order will not be made to take effect until after the defence has been delivered.

When, however, the order has been made, the next step will be for your opponent to comply with it by swearing what is called an affidavit of documents.

Order XXXI., Rule 13   The affidavit to be made by a party against whom such order as is mentioned in the last preceding Rule has been made, shall specify which, if any, of the documents therein mentioned he objects to produce, and it shall be in the Form No. 8 in Appendix B, with such variations as circumstances may require (*vide* App. No. 1, p. 171).

In this affidavit your opponent is required to state:—

(i.) What documents relating to the matters in question are in his possession or power.

(ii.) Whether he objects to produce any of them, and if so, on what ground (*i.e.*, if privilege, for instance, is claimed).

(iii.) What relevant documents he has had in his possession or power and when they were last so, and what has become of them and in whose possession they are.

(iv.) That he has not, and never had, any other relevant documents in his possession or power.

Armed with this information, the solicitor instructing you will now be enabled to inspect the documents for which no privilege has been claimed and to take copies of them, under Rule 15 of Order XXXI., which is as follows :—

15. Every party to a cause or matter shall be entitled, at any time by notice in writing to give notice to any other party in whose

pleadings or affidavits reference is made to any document, to produce such document for the inspection of the party giving such notice, or of his solicitor, and to permit him or them to take copies thereof, and any party not complying with such notice shall not afterwards be at liberty to put any such document in evidence on his behalf in such cause or matter unless he shall satisfy the Court or a Judge that such document relates only to his own title, he being a defendant to a cause or matter, or that he had some other cause or excuse which the Court or Judge shall deem sufficient for not complying with such notice, in which case the Court or Judge may allow the same to be put in evidence on such terms as to costs and otherwise as the Court or Judge shall think fit.

Although the Rules thus provide a specific penalty for failure to produce a document after notice, no penalty is actually laid down for failure to disclose a document in the affidavit of documents. But such an omission, apart from being perjury, would, of course, form the subject of cross-examination and comment, and if it resulted in surprise or hardship might very well be a ground for refusing a successful party costs.

The form of this notice is provided for in Rule 16 of the same Order, which is as follows ·—

Notice to any party to produce any documents referred to in his pleading or affidavits shall be in Form No 9 in Appendix B, with such variations as circumstances may require (*vide post*, App. No. 2, p. 171).

And Rule 17 provides that :—

The party to whom such notice is given shall within two days from the receipt of such notice, if all the documents therein referred to have been set forth by him in such affidavit as is mentioned in Rule 13, or if any of the documents referred to in such notice have not been set forth by him in any such affidavit within four days from the receipt of such notice, deliver to the party giving the same a notice stating a time within three days from the delivery thereof at which the documents, or such of them as he does not object to produce, may be inspected at the office of his solicitor, or in the case of bankers' books or other books of account, or books in constant use for the purposes of any trade or business, at their usual place of custody, and stating which (if any) of the documents he objects to produce and on what ground. Such notice shall be in the Form No. 10, Appendix B, with such variations as circumstances may require (*vide post*, App. No. 3, p 172).

In case your opponent still places difficulties in the way, you may apply to the Master under Rule 18 (1), which is as follows :—

18 (1). If a party served with notice under Rule 17 [*sic*] omits to give such notice of a time for inspection or objects to give inspection, or offers inspection elsewhere than at the office of his solicitor, the Court or Judge may on the application of the party desiring it, make an order for inspection in such place and in such manner as he may think fit. Provided the order shall not be made when and so far as the Court or a Judge shall be of opinion that it is not necessary either for disposing fairly of the cause or matter or for saving costs

On the other hand, it may be that the matter is one within a small scope, that there has been little or no correspondence between the parties, or that the only documents which you wish to inspect are documents which have been already referred to in your opponent's pleadings or in some affidavit which he has sworn in the course of the action

In that case there is no necessity to apply under Rule 12 (*vide ante*) for an affidavit of documents to be made by your opponent. So far as documents which are mentioned in your opponent's pleadings and affidavits are concerned, you can give him notice without further ado to produce them for your inspection, under Rules 15, 16, and 17, and if necessary get an order under Rule 18 (1).

So, too, if you are already sufficiently informed as to the nature of the material documents in your opponent's possession to be able to specify them, you may swear an affidavit and apply to the Master for an order to inspect the documents under Rule 18 (2), or Rule 19A (3), which are as follows :—

Rule 18 (2). Any application to inspect documents, except such as are referred to in the pleadings, particulars, or affidavits of the party against whom the application is made or disclosed in his affidavit of documents, shall be founded upon an affidavit showing of what documents inspection is sought, that the party applying is entitled to inspect them, and that they are in the possession or power of the other party. The Court or Judge shall not make such order for inspection of such documents when and so far as the Court or Judge shall be of opinion that it is not necessary either for disposing fairly of the cause or matter or for saving costs.

Rule 19A (3). The Court or a Judge may, on the application of any party to a cause or matter at any time, whether an affidavit of documents shall or shall not have already been ordered or made, make an order requiring any other party to state by affidavit whether any one or more specific documents, to be specified in the application, is or are, or has or have at any time been in his possession or power; and, if not then in his possession, when he parted with the same, and what has become thereof. Such application shall be made on an affidavit stating that in the belief of the deponent the party against whom the application is made has, or has at some time had in his possession or power the document or documents specified in the application, and that they relate to the matters in question in the cause or matter, or to some of them.

The latter Rule is more especially applicable to those cases in which your opponent has omitted reference to a particular document in his affidavit of documents, or has denied that a particular document is in his possession or power.

Finally, the Master has the power of requiring the production of any material document on oath, at any stage of the proceedings, by virtue of Rule 14 of Order XXXI.

Rule 14. It shall be lawful for the Court or a Judge, at any time during the pendency of any cause or matter, to order the production by any party thereto, upon oath, of such of the documents in his possession or power, relating to any matter in question in such cause or matter as the Court or Judge shall think right, and the Court may deal with such documents, when produced, in such manner as shall appear just

When the solicitor instructing you has thus inspected and taken copies of the documents in your opponent's possession, and so prevented your being surprised by the production at the trial of unexpected documentary evidence, your next step will be to ensure that you shall be able to give evidence at the trial of the original documents in your opponent's possession, which assist your case.

For the above-mentioned rules and notices apply only to the production of documents for your solicitor's inspection, and not to production at the trial.

R. S. C., Order XXXII., Rule 8, is as follows :—

Notice to produce documents shall be in the Form No. 14 in Appendix B with such variations as circumstances may require. An affidavit of the solicitor, or his clerk, of the service of any notice to produce, and of the time when it was served, with a copy of the notice to produce, shall in all cases be sufficient evidence of the service of the notice, and of the time when it was served *vide post*, App. No. 4, p. 172).

The result of giving this notice will be, that if your opponent refuses or neglects to produce the original documents, you will b abled, on proof of the notice, and that the docume. ire in his possession, to give secondary evidence of them.

At the same time, in order to save the expense and trouble of proving your own original documents, your solicitor client will probably serve a notice on the other side to admit your own original documents under the following Rules :—

Order XXXII., Rule 2. Either party may call upon the other party to admit any document, saving all just exceptions ; and in case refusal or neglect to admit, after such notice, the costs of ι ing any such document shall be paid by the party so neglecting or refusing, whatever the result of the cause or matter may be, unles t the trial or hearing the Court or a Judge shall certify that the refusal to admit was reasonable ; and no costs of proving any document shall be allowed unless such notice be given, except where omission to the notice is, in the opinion of the taxing officer, a saving of nse.

Rule 3. A notice to admit documents shall be in the Form No. 11 in Appendix B, with such variations as circumstances may require (*vide post*, App. No. 5, p. 172).

Rule 7. An affidavit of the solicitor or his clerk, of the due signature of any admissions made in pursuance of any notice to admit documents or facts, shall be sufficient evidence of such admissions, if evidence thereof be required.

So far we have dealt only with documents in the power or possession of your opponent. But it will be remembered that in the affidavit of documents (provided your opponent has made one) your opponent was required to state what had become of material documents, which were no longer in his possession.

Should any of the documents, so referred to, be necessary to your case, it will be advisable to serve on the person in whose possession they now are a *subpœna duces tecum.*

And the same applies to any other person who is in possession of documents, on which you intend to rely at the trial; unless, of course, you have reason to know that he will attend without a subpœna.

But it is not only in respect of documentary evidence that you can fortify your evidence before going into Court by a judicious application of the Rules of the Supreme Court. Admissions of fact can also be obtained in two different ways.

There may be facts which, though put in issue on the pleadings, yet are not likely to be contested at the trial. Or there may be facts which are common ground to both parties, and yet will be expensive to prove. If the onus of proving such facts be on your shoulders, you will be able to save the expense of proving them by giving the other side notice to admit them under Order XXXII., Rule 4. (For the form of notice, *vide post*, App. No. 6, p. 173.)

Or, again, there may be facts which you think your opponent would be unlikely to deny on oath, or as to which it is important that you should know on oath what answer he will make.

In such a case you may interrogate your opponent on oath by virtue of Order XXXI. of the Rules of the Supreme Court, provided you get the leave of a Master.

Order XXXI., Rule 1. In any cause or matter, the plaintiff or defendant, by leave of the Court or a Judge, may deliver interrogatories in writing for the examination of the opposite parties, or any one or more of such parties, and such interrogatories when delivered shall have a note at the foot thereof, stating which of such inter-

rogatories each of such persons is required to answer: Provided
that no party shall deliver more than one set of interrogatories to
the same party without an order for that purpose: Provided also
that interrogatories which do not relate to any matter in question
in the cause or matter shall be deemed irrelevant, notwithstanding
that they might be admissible on the oral cross-examination of a
witness.

Rule 2.   On an application for leave to deliver interrogatories
the particular interrogatories proposed to be delivered shall be
submitted to the Court or Judge.   In deciding upon such application, the Court or Judge shall take into account any offer which
may be made by the party sought to be interrogated, to deliver
particulars, or to make admissions, or to produce documents
relating to the matter in question, or any of them, and leave shall
be given as to such only of the interrogatories submitted as the
Court or Judge shall consider necessary either for disposing fairly
of the cause or matter or for saving costs.

Rule 4.   Interrogatories shall be in the Form No. 6 in Appendix B, with such variations as circumstances may require (vide
post, App. No 7, p. 173).

Rule 6   Any objection to answering any one or more of several
interrogatories on the ground that it or they is or are scandalous
or irrelevant, or not bonâ fide for the purpose of the cause or
matter, or that the matters inquired into are not sufficiently
material at that stage, or on any other ground, may be taken in
the affidavit in answer.

Rule 7.   Any interrogatories may be set aside on the ground
that they have been exhibited unreasonably or vexatiously, or
struck out on the ground that they are prolix, oppressive, unnecessary, or scandalous, and any application for this purpose
may be made within seven days after service of the interrogatories.

Rule 8.   Interrogatories shall be answered by affidavit to be
filed within ten days, or within such other time as the Judge may
allow

Rule 10.   No exception shall be taken to any affidavit in answer,
but the sufficiency or otherwise of any such affidavit objected to
as insufficient shall be determined by the Court or a Judge on
motion or summons.

Rule 11.   If any person interrogated omits to answer, or answers
insufficiently, the party interrogating may apply to the Court or a
Judge for an order requiring him to answer, or to answer further,
as the case may be.   And an order may be made requiring him to
answer or answer further, either by affidavit or by vivâ voce
examination, as the Judge may direct.

By means of a successful interrogation you may either

obtain some useful admissions of fact, or at any rate obtain useful information as to the case you will have to meet at the trial.

There is another preliminary matter which is so important to the success or failure of the evidence in Court, that it must be referred to : that is, counsel's Advice on evidence.

The object of Advice on evidence is that the solicitor instructing you should know exactly what evidence will be necessary in Court.

Bearing this in mind, you will ascertain from the pleadings, documents and interrogatories, exactly what are the issues between the parties, and on whom the onus of proof in respect of each issue lies.

This, too, will be a convenient moment for making up your mind as to which party has the right to begin. Generally speaking, this is an advantage, and should therefore be claimed. It will depend on the pleadings, the general rule being that that party has the right to begin, which, in the absence of proof, would substantially fail in the action.*

Having set out the issues and the onus of proof in each case, you will then, from the facts and documentary evidence at your disposal, proceed to detail the witnesses or other evidence necessary to prove or rebut in each issue.

With regard to documentary evidence, something has been said above. Ordinarily a document can only be proved by production of the original. If, however, your opponent fails to comply with your notice to produce originals in his possession, you may prove them by secondary evidence. And there are certain classes of documents which, either at common law or by statute, may be proved by the production of copies.

These copies are either (i.) office copies, or (ii.) examined copies, or (iii.) certified copies.† It will, therefore, be

* Thus, if the damages be unliquidated, this alone will entitle the plaintiff to begin. *Mercer v. Whall*, 5 Q. B. 447.
† For a description of these various kinds of copies, and the documents

necessary for you to advise which, if any, of these three kinds of copies will be the appropriate method of proving any particular document.

In addition to the preliminary steps, which have been dealt with above, it may be expedient for the advocate to fortify his case by evidence taken on Commission, before the trial. This is provided for by Order XXXVII., Rule 5 :—

"The Court or a Judge may in any cause or matter where it shall appear necessary for the purposes of justice make any order for the examination upon oath before the Court or Judge, or any officer of the Court, or any other person and at any place of any witness or person, and may empower any party to any such cause or matter to give such deposition in evidence therein, on such terms, if any, as the Court or a Judge may direct."

Thus, if one of your witnesses is too unwell to attend at the trial, or intends to leave the country before the trial, you may apply by summons for an order for a Commission to examine him.

Similarly, if witnesses or the parties reside abroad, you may apply for an order for a Commission or for Letters of Request, to examine them abroad.

The distinction between a Commission and Letters of Request is that, whereas in the former the examination is conducted by officers appointed by the English Courts, in the case of the latter the examination is conducted through the judicature of the foreign country. And in the case of countries which, like Germany, object to the issuing of a Commission, Letters of Request must be resorted to.

The granting or withholding of orders for Commissions and Letters of Request is discretionary, and, so far as parties are concerned, an order will be more readily obtained for the examination of a defendant, than of a plaintiff, resident abroad. The details of the practice and the forms will be found in the Annual and Yearly Practices, under Order XXXVII., Rules 5, 6, 6a.

to which they are appropriate, see Roscoe's Nisi Prius Evidence, 18th ed., p. 96 *et seq.*, Best, p. 401 *et seq.*

CHAPTER II.

EXAMINATION IN CHIEF.

GREAT care must be exercised by the advocate in the introduction of his evidence. As has been pointed out in the preceding chapter, he should, before he enters into the trial of the case, obtain from his adversary every lawful advantage to which he is entitled, so far as the production of documents is concerned, and in obtaining an admission of the genuineness of papers which he will find it necessary to introduce.

The advocate should pay great attention to the order in which he puts in his evidence. It is difficult to lay down general rules upon this subject, and much must depend upon the sound judgment of the advocate himself.

There are some suggestions which occur to us, however, which may prove helpful to the lawyer in court. Where the evidence is based upon documentary evidence, such as a bond, deed, or note, the first thing the plaintiff's attorney must do towards making out his case, is to produce and verify the paper, or account for its loss or absence, and prove its contents by secondary evidence (*vide ante*, p. 6, and *post*, p. 164). Formerly, if the document was subscribed by attesting witnesses, these witnesses had to be called, whether attestation were essential to the validity of the document or not. But now by s. 26 of the Common Law Procedure Act, 1854 (17 and 18 Vict. c. 125), "It shall not be necessary to prove by the attesting witness any instrument to the validity of which attestation is not requisite; and such instrument may be proved by admission, or otherwise, as if there had been no attesting witness thereto." Now, therefore, counsel will have to direct his attention to the question whether attestation is essential to the document in question. And this applies to criminal as well as to civil procedure (28 and 29 Vict. c. 18, s. 7).

If attestation is essential to the validity of the document, the attesting witnesses must still be called, or their absence satisfactorily accounted for,* and proof of their handwriting introduced, unless the document be admitted on the pleadings or elsewhere. If the paper, the contents of which is to be proved, is in the possession of the opposite party, evidence of its contents cannot be offered until such party has been notified and had an opportunity to produce it in Court (ante, p. 6).

When this has been done, or in cases not based on written documents, the advocate must call his witnesses to establish the facts upon which the one side or the other is to rely for a verdict.

The manner of putting in the testimony is of great importance, and will often tax the advocate to the utmost of his skill and sagacity. The arrangement of his testimony and the order in which he calls his witnesses will also demand much care and attention.

The advocate should, in nearly every case, put his most intelligent and most honest witness in the box first. It is necessary that a good impression should be made upon the Court and jury at the earliest possible moment. The first witness generally has to run the gauntlet of a sharp cross-examination, and if the first witness passes this creditably, he encourages the other witnesses on the same side, and makes a favourable impression upon the Court and jury which his adversary will find it difficult to eradicate.

---

* As to what is satisfactory, see Roscoe's Nisi Prius Evidence, 18th ed, p. 133   If the attesting witness denies the execution of the document, he may be cross examined, for he is deemed to be the witness of the Court, *Jones* v *Jones*, 24 T L R. 839 and the execution may, in this case, be proved *aliunde*. *Talbot* v. *Hodson*, 7 Taunt 251.

If he pursues another course, and is imprudent enough to place a weak, foolish, or timid witness in the box first, the witness may do incalculable harm to the cause of the party who introduced him.

It becomes necessary sometimes for the plaintiff only to put in enough of his evidence to make out a *primâ facie* case, and it is occasionally best to keep back the strongest testimony till the testimony of his opponent has been heard, and then offer it by way of rebuttal to the case which has been made against him.

After the jurors have heard the testimony for the defence they are better prepared than they were before to appreciate the remaining testimony of the plaintiff.

It is highly important for the advocate to call, in immediate connection with each other, all the witnesses to the same subject-matter so as to prevent the attention of the jury from being distracted by the introduction of different portions of the case which constitute new subjects, between the parts of what are properly related to each other.

The same may be said as to the introduction of the testimony for the defence. It should be introduced in the most orderly and regular manner: each portion of the case should be proved separately.

The advocate will find that it is a good plan also to save one of his best witnesses for the close of his case. It is as important to end well as to begin well, and, as a general rule, the same order should be observed in the introduction of testimony as in the arrangement of the arguments in a speech. Some of the best witnesses should be examined first and the others last, while the weak or foolish witnesses should be placed between.

Sometimes, however, the adversary's case should be anticipated and the jury prepared for it. This is the case where there is anything suspicious in appearance, which can be fully explained, and the opportunity which the plaintiff may have to tell his story first, without concealment or artifice, and corroborate it by the testimony of all his witnesses, should be improved.

The usual mode of proceeding, in our Courts, in ordinary cases, preparatory to the examination of a witness, is to swear him in chief. But if an objection is made as to his competency, he should be examined on the *voir dire*.

Since the abolition of incompetency on the ground of interest, infamy, and want of religious belief, the only grounds of incompetency are defect of understanding, and in criminal proceedings, that the party against whom the evidence is offered is the husband or wife of the witness.*

The question of competency is one for the decision of the Judge, and the inquiry may be by examination of the proposed witness on oath on the *voir dire*, or by sworn evidence *aliunde* (*vide* Archbold, Crim Plead, 23rd ed., p. 387) But where the incompetency arises from defect of understanding, as in the case of lunatics, idiots, young children, etc., the preliminary inquiry cannot, upon the *voir dire*, be upon oath so far as the proposed witness is concerned, for the reason that the very ground of incompetency assumes that the proposed witness has no perception of the obligation of an oath.

In the case of *The Queen* against *Hill*, 2 Den. 254;

---

* The position is now this :—In criminal cases by virtue of the Criminal Evidence Act, 1898 (61 & 62 Vict. c 36), s 1, the husband or wife of a prisoner is a competent witness *for the defence*, if called with the consent of the prisoner

But the prosecution may not call the husband or wife of the prisoner, except in the case of prisoners charged with offences under the Vagrancy Act, 1824, the Offences against the Person Act, 1861, ss. 48—55, the Married Women's Property Act, 1882, ss 12, 16, the Criminal Law Amendment Act, 1885, and the Prevention of Cruelty to Children Act, 1894, and in cases of the prisoner having assaulted, etc , his or her wife or husband

In civil cases the husbands and wives of parties to a suit are both competent and compellable to give evidence (Evidence Amendment Act, 1853 (16 & 17 Vict c 82), s 1)

But both in civil and criminal cases communications between husband and wife are privileged from disclosure in evidence , *vide* s 3 of that statute as to civil cases, and s 1 (d) of the Criminal Evidence Act, 1898 (61 & 62 Vict. c. 36), for criminal cases.

20 L. J. M. C. 222, a prisoner was indicted for manslaughter; he was an inmate of a lunatic asylum, and the principal witness against him was another inmate of the asylum, who was subject to a delusion that he had a number of spirits about him who were continually talking to him, but in other respects he appeared to be perfectly sane. He was examined at considerable length by the counsel for the prisoner before he was sworn, both as to the subject of his particular delusion, and also as to his religious belief, and having given a satisfactory statement on the latter point, he was sworn in chief, and gave a well-connected and rational account of a transaction relating to the charge in question, which he stated he himself witnessed.

Other witnesses were examined in this case, previously to the lunatic being called, to speak as to his sanity, in order to enable the Judge to determine as to his competency to testify; and the Court of Crown Cases Reserved held that this was the correct course, though when the witness was admitted, it was for the jury to determine whether his testimony was affected by his insanity, and what degree of weight was to be attached to it.

This case is important, also, as deciding that it is not every degree of mental imbecility which will render a person incompetent as a witness.

After a witness has been regularly sworn he is first examined by the party who produced him. Then the other party may cross-examine him, and then the party who called him may re-examine. This usually closes the examination of the witness, but the Court may order a witness to be recalled and examined or cross-examined at any stage of the trial.

The purpose of the examination in chief is to lay before the Court and the jury all that the witness knows about the case which is relevant and material, while it is the office of cross-examination to sift, and search, to correct and supply omissions, and the object of re-examination to explain, rectify, and put in order.

No better mode of ascertaining the truth of a past transaction will probably ever be devised by human ingenuity than the present method of *vivâ voce* examination of witnesses, conducted as it is in open Court, in the sight of the public and in the presence of the parties, their counsel, and of the Judge and jury, who all have an opportunity of observing the intelligence, demeanour, inclination, bias or prejudice of the witnesses. In this way every man is given a fair and impartial trial, and his rights cannot be abridged, nor he deprived of the inestimable blessings of life, liberty, or property, without the concurrence of Judge and jury. In all cases, too, he has the constitutional privilege of facing his accusers, and by a manly defence, of shaping public opinion, which in this enlightened day is one of the greatest safeguards against injustice of every kind.

The manner and deportment of witnesses, and the proper method of examining them in chief, is such an important subject, that we deem it expedient to give the following observations made by Mr. Evans, the learned editor of "Pothier on Obligations." The law of evidence has undergone some changes since these observations were penned, but the advocate will readily note the changes without having them pointed out.

We are inclined to believe that the advocate will be greatly benefited by an attentive perusal of the suggestions made by Mr. Evans :—

" The manner and deportment of witnesses is very commonly a principal ground of assent to, or dissent from their testimony ; and is doubtless a very natural indication of the existence or want of sincerity. That the disposition of the witness will have an influence on his manner is undisputed ; the adequate observation of it is, however, a matter requiring the most skilful and judicious discernment ; the detection of affected plausibility, and the assistance of constitutional timidity, are objects which respectively import, in an eminent degree, the proper administration of justice. A perfect judgment of the causes of a person's demeanour upon a particular occasion, can only be formed by those who have a previous knowledge of his general habits and character, and in this respect an intelligent jury is of great advantage ; since, being assembled from different parts of the country, some of them will, in most cases, have at least a general knowledge of the witnesses who appear before them. It would be greatly beyond the limits of my power to trace even a slight outline of this extensive subject, but a few detached observations, founded upon my impressions respecting it, may not be wholly irrelevant. In deciding upon the demeanour of a witness, considerable allowance is to be made for the unaccustomed situation in which he is placed, and the impressions which it may be calculated to make upon his mind. To some persons this public appearance is a matter of indifference, but by many it is regarded with an apprehension, productive of embarrass-ment and agitation, which to skilful observers may appear the result of insincerity. This embarrassment will sometimes attach itself in a peculiar degree to those who are accustomed to appear before the public in a different situation, and who are therefore habitually anxious respecting the impression which they may induce. It is an anecdote of Garrick, that when examined as a witness respecting the nature of a free benefit, he was incapable of giving an intelligible testimony. In deciding upon the demeanour of witnesses, much attention is due to the mode of interrogation and the popular opinion respecting the person who is engaged in it. An asperity in the peculiar conduct of the counsel, of the Judge, or even the reputation of it with respect to the former, will necessarily produce an effect upon the sensations and deportment of the witness , and an apprehension of the ridicule which frequently affixes itself permanently to the character, is often a predominant sensation of the witness upon his examination. Good sense, when fully exercised, will correct these apprehensions, and satisfy the witness that violence and ridicule will be ineffectual, when opposed to the plain and unaffected language of truth; but the dictates of good sense are often an insufficient preservative against constitutional timidity.

"A resolution to appear undaunted, and repel the expected aggression of counsel by insolence, a foolish inclination to make a theatrical exhibition of wit and humour, exciting the horse-laugh of the bystanders, a moroseness and sullenness of temper, will give an unfavourable aspect to the manner of a witness when there is no intentional want of veracity in the matter. The real absurdity of a witness's demeanour or mode of representation, will often diminish the impression of the facts for which it is necessary to resort to his testimony, and particularly in cases where there is a latitude of discretion, as in questions of damages, the judgment is often practically biassed by the sentiment of ridicule being a test of truth. A due regard to the principles of justice will, however, prevent the fair demands of a party from being affected by the sullenness or absurdity of the witnesses whom he is necessitated to adduce in support of it; and will lead the mind to a studious discrimination between the fact which is the subject of inquiry, and the accidental circumstances which may accompany the relation of it.

"The judgment of a witness's manner is not unfrequently formed by a contrast between a cool and steady narration, and a fluttering hesitation; this judgment may, however, often be fallacious, for a witness who has prepared his story, may have sufficiently arranged the particulars of it in his mind, while another who has had an opportunity of contradicting it, if false, is surprised and confounded by the unexpected statement. In a case where I had an opportunity of knowing the real facts I have seen a witness give a steady and collected representation of a supposed conversation in a perfectly simple and unaffected manner, the opposite witness, when suddenly interrogated as to the existence of such a conversation, began with, 'Not that I recollect, I do not believe it, upon my honour,' and a great many other exclamations in such a confused suspicious manner, that even those who, from their private knowledge, had the most indisputable confidence of the veracity with which he told them upon coming out of Court, that there was not a syllable of truth in the conversation related, perfectly acquiesced in the propriety of a decision founded upon the opinion of his falsehood.

"The following passage from a man of considerable ability is not inapplicable to the purpose of the present inquiry. After remarking that guilt is probably more daring than innocence, but the voice of innocence has greater *energy and more convincing powers*, the look of innocence is more serene and bright than that of the guilty liar, he states an instance of two young persons who more than once came before him and most solemnly affirmed, the one, 'Thou art the father of my child,' the other, 'I never had any knowledge of thee.' 'On the one hand,' says he, 'I beheld the persuasive look of innocence, the indescribable look that so expressively said, 'And darest thou deny it?' I beheld, on the contrary, a clouded and insolent look, I heard the rude, the loud voice of presumption, but which, like the look, was unconvincing, hollow, that with forced tones answered, 'Yes, I dare.' I viewed the manner of standing, the motion of the hands, and particularly the undecided step, and at the moment when I awfully described the solemnity of an oath, at that moment I saw, in the motion of the lips, the downcast look, the manner of standing of the one party, and the open, astonished, firm,

2—2

penetrating, warm, calm look, that silently exclaimed,
'Lord Jesus! and wilt thou swear?' I saw, I heard,
I felt guilt and innocence.

"That testimony is very open to suspicion, which is
given by a person who is evidently meditating upon the
materiality and tendency of his answer, before he will let
it be given, or, on the other hand, who bolts out with
precipitancy, before he hears the question, an answer
indicating a catechised preparation; the effect of either
of these circumstances singly is greatly increased by the
combination in different parts of the same testimony.
But even that previous study of an answer, which has
been mentioned, will have a different effect, according
to the character, and situation, and habits, of the person
who is examined. I have, in an earlier part of this
discussion, taken notice of circumstances calculated to
influence the disposition, and which, though by no means
justifying prevarication in any case, diminish the suspicion
of a want of substantial veracity, which results from a
want of propriety in incidental particulars   he suspicion of fabrication rises highest, when the witness is one
of those inferior retainers of the law, who are commonly
attendant upon courts of judicature, who have a cunning
acuteness in the observation of its proceedings, and who,
from their occupation, are frequently in the habit of
swearing to facts, in their own nature liable to misrepresentation, and placed beyond the reach of detection or
contradiction.

"The general character of witnesses is also a circumstance which has naturally a considerable influence upon
the credit of their testimony. . . . But, wherever there is
reasonable ground to suppose a bias in the mind, with
respect to the effect of the testimony, a previous criminality of conduct will very justly excite suspicions of its
veracity; and the mind will naturally refuse its assent
to declarations made by those whose disposition in
favour of the event cannot be supposed to be counter-

acted by a superior sense of obligation   I have already
observed, that to assent to a given proposition we require
a preponderance of testimony in support of it; in questions, therefore, respecting the credit of a witness, the
want of assent is not founded upon an assurance that
his testimony is false, but the want of an adequate
assurance that it is true.   Where it is distinctly ascertained that the witness is indifferent with respect to the
event, or where it appears that his wishes would naturally
incline to opposition to his testimony, the general inclination to veracity might be, in most cases, a sufficient
assurance of the facts deposed to by a person even of the
most exceptionable character; but the testimony will be
properly open to suspicion, not only when a person of
this description distinctly appears to have a collateral
motive for desiring a decision in support of his testimony,
but also whenever there is not a sufficient reason for
presuming the contrary; for the inducements which may
operate upon a mind susceptible of corrupt influence
cannot easily be detected, although they may actually
exist.   It is the want of an adequate assurance that
the testimony is true, which very properly occasions a
great degree of caution to be applied to the testimony of
accomplices in criminal prosecutions and induces Courts,
and juries, to disregard such testimony, except so far as
it is confirmed by circumstances affecting the parties
accused, deposed to by witnesses of irreproachable character.   There is not in these cases a positive suspicion
arising from the nature of the evidence itself, that it is
actually false; but there is a manifest want of those
principles of duty and obligation, which are the strongest
assurances of its being true; the actual motive is almost
always in favour of truth, if it be clear that the witness
had some companion in his offence; and it has not in
any instance occurred to me, to suspect that evidence of
this description which I have had an opportunity of
hearing, was fabricated; but there is no doubt that it

frequently might be so, if a less jealous caution was exercised in its reception.

" It is an established rule, that witnesses examined with a view to discredit the testimony of others, cannot be admitted to depose to particular facts of criminality, but can only express their general opinion, whether the party is or is not entitled to be believed upon his oath (*vide infra*, p. 169) ; but the other side, to support the testimony, may inquire what are the reasons of disbelief, which sometimes, as in a case above adverted to, are ridiculous enough.   If it is declined to inquire into these reasons, there is pretty considerable ground to presume a conscientiousness that the opinion is founded upon adequate motives.   I have heard witnesses asked, whether they had ever known the persons against whose veracity they depose, give false evidence in a Court of justice ; and upon their answering in the negative, it was intimated to the jury, that the testimony to their discredit was absolutely frivolous ; whereas, if the question had been, what were the reasons upon which the discredit was founded, a fraudulent conduct might have been shown which indicated the want of moral and religious principle, and consequently affected the strongest ground of reliance upon testimony. When witnesses speak to the character of others, not only their own character, but their ability, and opportunity to form an adequate judgment, are circumstances very proper to be taken into consideration.

" It is a rule of law that witnesses *cannot be asked** any questions which tend to subject themselves to punishment, *or as it is usually expressed, to criminate themselves ; but*

---

* *Semble* the rule of law is not, in England at any rate, that the witness may not be asked such questions, but that he is not obliged to answer them It is for the witness, and not for his counsel, to claim the privilege.   For a discussion of the authorities, *vide* Archbold, Crim Plead , 23rd ed , p 399, Roscoe's Nisi Prius Evidence, 18th ed , p 168, Best, 10th ed , p 114.

It must be remembered that this rule does not extend to prevent a prisoner who is giving evidence on his own behalf from being asked and compelled to answer questions tending to show that he committed the offence with which he is then charged, or other offences (provided they are material under the Criminal Evidence Act, 1898, s 1 (f)) *whether they may be asked if they have already received a punishment, which does not disqualify their testimony, or whether they may be interrogated as to any circumstances of improper conduct, not immediately connected with the subject of their examination, and also, whether their refusal to answer inquiries upon these subjects can be observed upon as affecting the credit of their testimony, are questions of great importance upon which there is a very considerable difference of opinion. Some judges are very strongly of opinion, that these inquiries ought not to be allowed; but it has been understood to be the more prevalent opinion, and is clearly supported by the course of practice which has actually prevailed that these inquiries should be admitted. Mr. Peake, in the second edition of his ' Law of Evidence,' states the argument in support of these opposite opinions, in a very fair and perspicuous manner; and the right and propriety of the examination alluded to are maintained with considerable ability in a pamphlet entitled, 'An Argument in favour of the rights of Cross-Examination.' I have at all times felt a very considerable difficulty in the consideration of this subject, but as a knowledge of a witness's habits and pursuits, his conduct and disposition, will naturally influence the regard which is paid to his assertions, I think that the preponderance of argument is in favour of the opinion, that an examination, by which these may be ascertained cannot, upon any general principles, be suppressed as irrelevant or improper; and that those arguments respecting a witness's conduct ought not to be rejected, which may tend to terminate the regard that the mind, without reference to technical rules or legal considerations, would pay to his testimony.** *

At the same time, I think that this is a liberty which,

---

* These are matters of cross-examination rather than of examination in chief, and are dealt with *post*, pp 64—70.

So far as previous convictions are concerned, the law in England is now settled by statute. In civil cases, s. 25 of the Common Law Procedure Act, 1854, and in criminal cases, s 6 of the Criminal Procedure Act, 1865, "Mr. Denman's Act," provided that witnesses may be asked

like all others, will be best secured by a cautious vigilance in repressing its abuse, by refusal of advocates to
adopt the passions and prejudices of their clients, and to
injure a witness by reproaches and insinuations, that
cannot reasonably be expected to influence the fair
decision of the cause; and by the Court showing a
marked discountenance to the adoption of a different
line of conduct, calculated only to occasion an unnecessary pain and injury to the witness, without promoting
the right or interests of the party.

"The situation of a witness in life is also a circumstance which frequently influences the regard that is paid
to his testimony, especially with respect to matters of
judgment and observation; and even with respect to
mere veracity it is not wholly indifferent, for although,
in the abstract, the testimony of every person is to be
regarded as true, and the same obligation may be equally
strong in every condition of society, the temporal disadvantages arising from the detection of falsehood or
prevarication, independent of the terrors of legal punishment, will frequently depend upon, or be connected with,
a person's rank and station; and therefore all considerations of credit, connected with the evidence itself, will
be, and constantly are, materially influenced by this
circumstance. The effect of a bias in favour of the
event of a cause, resulting from the situation of a witness,

---

whether they have been previously convicted, and unless they admit such
convictions, proof may be offered of them by certificate

Questions as to improper conduct by the witness may also be put, even
though the conduct in question has nothing to do with the matter at issue
in the case; and such questions must be answered The proper test of
whether such questions should be allowed by the judge would seem to be
this —Will the answer throw any light on the credibility of the witness?
If it will not, then the question ought not to be allowed, if it is otherwise
immaterial to the case.

But if questions as to improper conduct apart from the case itself are
put to a witness, merely for the sake of discrediting him, his answer must
be taken Evidence may not be called to contradict him For this
purpose improper conduct is different from a previous conviction; *cf. post*,
pp 64, 65

In criminal cases, prisoners called in their own defence may in general
not be asked such questions, *vide post*, pp. 65, 170.

will be more or less strong in proportion to his being more or less subject to temptation; the comparison between the relation itself and its probability, will be made with greater minuteness, in proportion to the stake in society which is engaged in support of its veracity. The influence of situation is most strong in cases of conflicting testimony; for supposing other circumstances to be equal in every respect, there is no doubt but that a considerable diversity of situation would have considerable influence in directing the balance of credit, and to illustrate the position of an extreme instance, few persons would hesitate in regarding the narrative of a clergyman on the one side, with superior credit, to that of a bailiff's follower on the other.

"The number of witnesses, and their concurrence in support of a given assertion, is also subject of material importance in deciding upon the credit of their testimony, because of the improbability of two witnesses concurring in the same falsehood or mistake of either of them individually; and the improbability increases in proportion with the number. But in the contrasting of contradictory testimony, the mere consideration of number is held subordinate to that of the indications of individual veracity, and the maxim that *ponderantur, non numerantur testes*, is of very frequent practical application. Other circumstances being equal, the preponderance of numbers is certainly entitled to the advantage, and sometimes this preponderance will be sufficiently great to counterbalance an apparent superiority in other circumstances on the opposite side, and although nothing can be more remote from the subject under discussion than the application of the strict rules of mathematical equality or proportion, a fair attention to the principles of those rules is often of considerable importance. The degree of influence or indifference of the respective witnesses to their apparent veracity, their demeanour, their character, their situation, the probability of their relation, are circumstances, all of

which are to be carefully and attentively brought into
the account. The opportunity of confederacy, or the
want of such opportunity, is a most important consideration in determining the effect of numbers. The concurrence in speaking of one observation of one detached
fact, is of much inferior value to the concurrence of persons speaking from detached and separate observations
of different facts leading to the same conclusion. I have
already had occasion to advert to the accordance or
variation of witnesses speaking of the same occurrence,
to the difference between that inconsistency which
essentially fastens itself upon the substance of the relation, and that which may be fairly referable to different
degrees of accuracy or minuteness, in the observation
or memory of facts which have actually occurred ; and
to the unity and accordance, which, being too strict and
circumstantial, are inconsistent with that diversity of
observation and expression that naturally occurs in the
unprepared account of a real transaction, and afford an
indication of concert and design. It is not an unfrequent observation that if one of the witnesses in support
of a cause is not entitled to be credited, the discredit
attaches to the cause and extends to other witnesses
apparently unexceptionable. This kind of objection is, I
think, sometimes applied too generally, and without using
that caution and discrimination which the principle of it
essentially requires. In case the impeachment of the
veracity of a particular witness results from circumstances that indicate management and fabrication in the
cause itself; in case the perjury of the witness implies
the subornation of the party, the whole system may be
regarded as tainted and corrupt, unless there are in any
other respects, superior reasons for believing the contrary ;
and the mere absence of circumstances of suspicion,
directly affecting the other witnesses, will not destroy the
presumption of falsity that has attached itself to the cause.
But if the imputation upon the particular witness is

merely personal; if it results in consideration foreign
to the immediate cause , if it is founded upon some collateral motive of his own, and no suspicion of subornation can be fairly entertained , the cause in other
respects should be at liberty to stand or fall upon its
general merits, without being affected upon the peculiar
objection , in the same manner as a series of reasoning,
in itself perfect and complete, is not affected by the
collateral of an untenable argument.

"The conflict of opposite witnesses is the grand source
of forensic altercation. In adverting to the circumstances which influence the credit of witnesses individually
or collectively, I have necessarily had occasion to mention
their opposition. Without going through the particulars
again, it will be sufficient, generally, to observe that
whatever principles of reasoning are correct and proper
when examining the veracity or accuracy of an individual
witness or a number of witnesses uncontradicted, become
more peculiarly important in determining the balance of
credit, with respect to veracity, or the superior degree of
accuracy, upon matters of judgment and observation, in
cases of conflict and opposition. The general ground of
credit, founded upon the presumption that a witness
speaks with truth and accuracy, is destroyed, when the
respective assertions are in opposition to each other, and
therefore cannot be both true. Whatever, therefore, may
establish or diminish the confidence in a witness, whose
testimony is uncontradicted, will determine the preference
in cases of opposition ; but the respective grounds of
assent or discredit are sometimes so equally balanced,
that the mind cannot, with satisfaction, pronounce a
judgment between them , and all that can be recommended is a calm, patient, and anxious investigation.
Where the possibility of mistake on the one side is contrasted with the imputation of perjury on the other, and
there are no collateral circumstances to fix the determination, there can be no doubt but that a casual error is to be

deemed more probable than a wilful misrepresentation.
When the judgment, after every exertion, is reduced to
the necessity of deciding, that on the one side or the
other, there has been an intentional falsehood, and no
satisfactory reasons occur for fixing the superiority of
credit; the last resource is to obliterate wholly the
conflicting testimony, and to determine upon the want of
a preponderance in proof, according to the rule which
must have prevailed in the total absence of it.   The
result of an investigation of evidence will, after the most
enlightened and painful research, be, in many cases,
unfortunately at variance with the actual truth, but in
proportion to the dangers of error inherent in the very
frame and nature of the subject, should be the care and
anxiety exercised in the avoidance of such error as may
proceed from an excess of confidence on the one hand or
of caution on the other, and although that care and
anxiety will often fail in their particular application, the
perfection of human precaution will be attained, if they are
so conducted that according to the principles of reason and
experience, they may be expected in general to succeed.

"To the above observations, in which I have endeavoured to sketch some of the principles that may not be
undeserving attention, in forming a judgment upon the
accuracy and veracity of evidence, and which are deduced
from the nature of the subject itself, it remains to subjoin
a few others, originally founded upon the same principles,
but more immediately connected with positive rules of
practical authority.   In the examination of witnesses, a
distinction is made with respect to the party by whom
they are called, it being, in general, inadmissible for a
party to put what are termed leading questions to the
witnesses adduced by himself, although such questions
are perfectly allowable upon a cross-examination.   It is
sometimes laid down that leading questions are those
which are to be answered by a mere affirmative or
negative, and in which, consequently, the answer is fully

suggested by the question. I think, however, that this description, and the objection founded upon it, are sometimes applied more extensively than the principle upon which they are founded requires, the good sense of the rule is perfectly manifest, with respect to all cases where the question propounded involves an answer immediately bearing upon the merits of the cause, and indicating to the witness a representation which will best accord with the interests of the party; but where the questions are merely introductory, where the mere answer yes or no, will leave the point of the case precisely as it found it, and can only be material as laying the foundation for a further inquiry, the reason of the objection does not occur, and the objection itself appears to be ill-founded; and the making it can only proceed from a captious and petulant disposition to interrupt the course of examination. If a witness is asked generally with reference to a particular occasion, whether a person said anything, the answer yes or no, cannot very materially advance the interest of the party; and can only serve as the foundation for the more general question, of what it was that was said. But I have very frequently known this preliminary question excite a clamorous interposition for correcting the supposed impropriety, by telling the advocate that his question should be, What did the person say? A question which necessarily supposes the existence of the general fact of something having been said, which possibly may not be the fact. I think that, according to the principles of good sense and fair reasoning, the restriction ought not to be extended to cases to which the occasion of it cannot be deemed to apply, and that if the question does not prompt an answer bearing upon the subject in dispute, if the negative or affirmative answer will be perfectly indifferent, except as serving for a foundation of further inquiry, the Court would best consult the ends of justice, by discouraging a conduct that can have no other effect than a frivolous altercation, distracting the attention of the advocate on the one side, and giving the other an opportunity of showing off his talents for interruption, and exhibiting a pertness which may impress the bystanders with an idea of spirit and ingenuity.

"It is said, that if a witness deposes falsely in any part of his testimony, the whole of it is to be rejected, and this is certainly correct so far as the falsehood supposes the guilt of perjury, the ground of credit being there destroyed, but if nothing can be imputed to a witness but error, inaccuracy, or embarrassment; if there does not appear to be a real intention to deceive or misrepresent; neither the objection nor the reason for it applies. The argument is sometimes urged with considerable vehemence, that a party who relies upon the testimony of a witness, must take it altogether, and cannot rely upon the one part and reject the other, whereas there is no inconsistency in asserting the general veracity of a narrative, and contending for the inaccuracy of some of its incidental particulars; much less is a party to be driven from his reliance upon the matters of fact related by a witness, because he contends that the witness is ill-founded in his reasonings and inferences deduced from them, as I have endeavoured to illustrate in a preceding part of the present section.*

"It is a general rule that a party cannot call witnesses to the discredit of others, whom he has before examined; but if a witness proves facts in a cause which make against the party who calls him, that party, as well as the other, may call other witnesses to contradict him as to those facts; for such facts are evidence in the cause, and the other witnesses are not called directly to discredit the first, but the impeachment of his credit is incidental and

* In *Bradley* v *Ricardo*, 8 Bing 57, the view contended for by Mr Evans was upheld, and it was said that where a party called other witnesses to contradict his own witness as to some particular fact, the rest of the evidence of the contradicted witness was not on that account to be rejected But Lord Campbell, C J, took a different view in the case of *Faulkner* v. *Brine*, 1 F & F. 255

consequential only. (Bull. 297, Peake 126.)* I think it probable that an exception would be allowed to the rule of exclusion above mentioned, in the case of instrumental witnesses denying their attestation ; for as these are witnesses whom it is necessarily incumbent on the party to produce, and the nature of their testimony is attended with suspicion, the discredit of their characters is a strong corroboration of the evidence, which it is competent to give from other sources, of the authenticity of the instrument (*vide supra*, p 12, note)

"An exception to the restriction above mentioned, against putting leading questions, is allowed in the case of witnesses appearing to be unwilling† to depose the truth in favour of the party by whom they are adduced. This unwillingness is commonly to be decided by the Judge, according to his impression of the demeanour of the witness upon the trial. The situation of the witness, and the inducements which he may have for withholding a fair account, are also very proper circumstances to be taken into consideration in forming this decision. A son will not be very forward in stating the misconduct of his father of which he has been the only witness : a servant will not, in an action against his master, be very ready to acknowledge the negligence committed by himself. I conceive that the principle which requires a party to abide by the whole of what his own witness has

* The procedure in such a case is, in England, now governed by statute The Criminal Procedure Act, 1865, s 3 (re enacting the Common Law Procedure Act, 1854, s. 22), now provides that in both civil and criminal cases —"A party producing a witness shall not be allowed to impeach his credit by general evidence of bad character, but he may, in case the witness shall, in the opinion of the Judge, prove adverse, contradict him by other evidence, or by leave of the Judge prove that he has made at other times a statement inconsistent with his present testimony ; but before such last mentioned proof can be given the circumstances of the supposed statement, sufficient to designate the particular occasion, must be mentioned to the witness, and he must be asked whether or not he has made such statement.

† In England the witness must be something more than unwilling, it would seem. He must be hostile, in the opinion of the Judge · *Bastin* v. *Carew*, Ry. & M 127, *Price* v. *Manning*, 42 Ch D 372, *Coles* v *Coles*, L. R 1 P. & M. 70, *vide* Roscoe's Nisi Prius Evidence. 18th ed pp 167 and 178, and cf. pp 35, 39, 164, *post.*

sworn or wholly to abandon it, is also, in this case, subject to an exception; for there certainly is no testimony, the veracity of which is less suspicious, than the admission extorted from any unwilling witness; and it would materially prejudice the interest of justice, if a witness of this description could place the party producing him in the dilemma of either abandoning the benefit of the truth which has been with difficulty obtained, or of adopting all the falsehood which the witness may have the iniquity to mix up with it.   The proper course seems to be to regard the evidence of an unwilling witness in the same light as that of a witness adduced by the adverse party, respecting which it is a settled principle, that you may believe what makes against his point who swears, without believing what makes for it.   *Bermon* v. *Woodbridge*, Doug. 781."

*   *   *   *   *

In some cases it is advisable to examine witnesses separately, and out of the hearing of each other.   The purpose of this separate examination of witnesses is to prevent, if possible, the danger of a concerted story among them, and to prevent the influence which the account given by one may have upon another.

Upon the application of counsel, in order to effect the purpose mentioned, the Judge will order the witnesses on both sides to withdraw at any stage of the proceedings. *Southey* v. *Nash*, 7 C. and P. 632   It is a matter of some doubt as to the absolute right in civil cases of one party to have these witnesses excluded from the Court-room, but it has been the practice both in the United States and in England for the Judge at the request of counsel on either side to order the exclusion of the witnesses, and we are of the opinion that an application of this kind should never be refused, unless for the very best reasons.

If any of the witnesses remain in Court after the Judge has ordered their withdrawal, they may be fined for contempt.   *Cobbett* v. *Hudson*, 1 E. and B. 14.

In the Exchequer Division it was said to be an inflexible rule that any witness who remained in Court after an order to withdraw, could not on any account be examined. *Att.-Gen.* v. *Bulpit*, 9 Price, 4.

And in the other Courts it was from time to time held that the admission or rejection of evidence under these circumstances was a matter within the discretion of the Court. *Parker* v. *M'William*, 6 Bing. 683; *Beamon* v. *Ellice*, 4 C. and P. 585.

But the better opinion would now seem to be that the Judge may not (except possibly in Revenue cases, under the old Exchequer Rule) refuse to admit the evidence of a witness under these circumstances. He may fine or commit the witness for contempt, and the disobedience of the witness may well become the subject of comment and remark. *Chandler* v. *Horne*, 2 Mood. and Rob. 423; *Cobbett* v. *Hudson*, 1 E. and B. 11, at p. 14.

The tendency in modern times is to turn on all the light. The civil law abounded in restrictions upon testimony, and one of the principal evidentiary rules laid down by it is that evidence should be *excluded* whenever any possible motive could operate to produce falsehood; hence it extended its prohibition to testify to relations within a certain degree, such as parent and child, and to the domestic relation of master and servant, to freedmen and clients, advocates, attorneys, tutors, curators, and those who, by eating, drinking, etc., with the other party, had thrown themselves open to the suspicion of subornation. But great discretion was given to the Judge in admitting and excluding testimony, and in judging its weight.

And formerly in England, when juries were composed of rude and illiterate men, a system of excluding testimony extremely technical and artificial, grew up

But when jurors became more capable of exercising their functions intelligently, the Judges began to open wide the door, until now they may be said to have taken it off the hinges, to let in all facts calculated to affect the minds of the jury in arriving at a correct conclusion.

In examination of a party's own witnesses, leading questions—that is, such as are calculated to instruct the witness how to answer on material points—are not allowed. This rule is based partly on the supposition that the witness is favourable to the party who calls him, consequently it is relaxed whenever it appears to the satisfaction of the Court that the witness is hostile, or that a more searching examination is necessary to elicit the truth.

The presumption is that a party who has an opportunity before trial to examine his witnesses, will only introduce those favourable to him, and in practice this is generally found to be the case; but of course there are exceptions, and it sometimes becomes necessary for the party to a cause to introduce, in his behalf, a witness who is extremely hostile to him.

The advocate should particularly guard against leading questions asked by his opponent, when the object of inquiry is to obtain the exact details of an admission, or of a conversation or agreement, and upon objection duly made the Courts in such cases are more rigorous in confining the direct examination to its strict rules.

But questions are objectionable as leading, not only when they directly suggest the answer which counsel examining desires, but they are also objectionable when they embody a material fact, and may be answered ·"yes," or "no," though neither is directly suggested.

The reason leading questions are excluded is founded in reason and common sense. Evidence extracted from a witness by skilfully arranged questions, contrived by counsel for the purpose of meeting his theory of the case, is very different, usually, from the genuine *unassisted* testimony of the same witness if left to tell his own story in his own way.

But great discretion is vested in the Courts in allowing

leading questions, and where the examination in chief has been regularly conducted, but the witness has inadvertently omitted some material fact, the Court will, generally, allow the counsel examining the witness to suggest to him the omitted fact, provided there is nothing in the surrounding circumstances calculated to arouse the suspicion that the witness was corrupt and his testimony false.

Questions of a merely introductory character, upon immaterial matters, may be leading. By permitting leading questions under such circumstances the Courts save a great deal of time, and prevent examinations from being drawn out to an immoderate length.

Where it is clearly apparent that a witness is adverse, the Court will permit the examination in chief to assume the form of a cross-examination.

When a party puts a witness in the box, to a certain extent, he vouches for him, and he will not be permitted by the Court to impeach his general reputation for veracity, nor to impugn his credibility by general evidence tending to show him unworthy of belief. But in order to prevent a party from being imposed upon by an artful witness, as one in the pay of his adversary, the party introducing the witness may show that he has been taken by surprise by the evidence and that it is contrary to the statements made by the witness previous to the trial, provided that the Judge is of opinion that the witness is hostile, and gives permission to counsel to take this course (*vide ante*, p. 31, notes, and *post*, p. 164, note). Before this proof can be given, however, the circumstances of the supposed statements, sufficient to designate the particular occasion, must be mentioned to the witness, and he must be asked whether he made such statements and be allowed to explain them.

Witnesses are only allowed to testify to such facts as are within their knowledge, but they will be allowed to

refresh their recollections and assist their memories by
the use of any written instrument or memorandum, an
entry in a book, etc., which were made at the time (*vide
post*, p. 168).

Many practitioners entrust the important work of
examining the witnesses on their side to the junior
counsel in the case and apparently underrate its importance. David Paul Brown, one of the best advocates
America has produced, says upon this subject : " There
is often more eloquence, more mind, more knowledge of
human nature displayed in the examination of witnesses
than in the discussion of the cause to which their testimony relates. Evidence without argument is worth
much more than argument without evidence. In their
union they are irresistible."

Mr. Birrell, in his admirable biographical sketch of
Sir Frank Lockwood, quotes from the *Birmingham Daily
Post* an address made by that eminent law officer in
March, 1893, in which the following paragraph appears .—
" He believed that the examination of a witness in chief,
or the direct examination of witnesses, as it was called
in Ireland, was very much underrated in its significance
and its importance. If they had to examine a witness,
what they had got to do was to induce him to tell his
story in the most dramatic fashion, without exaggeration ;
they had got to get him, not to make a mere parrot-like
repetition of the proof, but to tell his own story as though
he were telling it for the first time—not as though it were
words learnt by heart—but if it were a plaintive story,
plaintively telling it. And they had got to assist him in
the difficult work. They had got to attract him to the
performance of his duty, but woe be to them if they
suggested to him the terms in which it was to be put.
They must avoid any suspicion of leading the witness
while all the time they were doing it. They knew
perfectly well the story that he was going to tell , but
they destroyed absolutely the effect if every minute they

were looking down at the paper on which his proof was written. It should appear to be a kind of spontaneous conversation between the counsel on the one hand and the witness on the other, the witness telling artlessly his simple tale, and the counsel almost appalled to hear of the iniquity under which his client had suffered. It was in this way, and in this way alone, that they could effectively examine a witness "

Sir James Scarlett, one of the most successful English advocates of modern times, attached great importance to the examination in chief, and would never delegate this trust to another lawyer in a case in which he appeared, but always examined his own witnesses in person.*

No lawyer can be successful in the highest sense of the term unless he is a master of the difficult art of examining witnesses. It requires a greater combination of qualities than almost any other branch of advocacy, the most important of which are patience, coolness, courage, and tact. It is extremely difficult to lay down rules for the performance of this difficult task. Much depends upon the good judgment and sagacity of the examiner. A few precepts, mainly gleaned from the writings on the subject of advocacy, together with some observations which are the result of experience, may, however, be of service.

It is safe to say at the beginning that no two witnesses can be treated exactly alike. The examiner must be governed to a great extent by the individuality and the peculiar idiosyncrasies of each witness. When the witness is timid or diffident the advocate should not at once proceed to the heart of his case, but should ask a few unimportant questions, such as, " What is your name ? " " What is your age ? " " Where do you reside ? " " What is your occupation ? " etc., until he becomes composed and self-possessed, for at the

* See, however, *post*, p. 51, for the usual practice.

beginning he is apt to be frightened and ill at ease. The advocate should speak kindly and reassuringly to a witness of this character, and if he neglects this precaution he will be apt to injure his case, for if the witness becomes confused he will be liable to say something which he did not intend to say, and thus damage the side for which he was called.

Before attempting to examine a witness the advocate should be well informed as to what the witness will swear.

In England, owing to the separation between the two branches of the profession, it is not the custom for the advocate to examine his witnesses before the trial, as it is in the United States. In England this is left to the solicitor.

And it is the generally accepted view of members of the English Bar that counsel should not meet the witnesses in conference before the trial, excepting of course the parties.

But the solicitor's position, as an intermediary between the lay client and counsel, should, it is suggested, be turned to the fullest account. And counsel should through the solicitor ascertain something of the weak and strong points of the witnesses whom he is going to examine.

Counsel should impress upon the solicitor the importance of selecting the best witnesses, where a selection is possible.

By the best we mean the most honest, intelligent, and the men of the best address. It often happens that a fact may be proved by a great many witnesses, and when this occurs a selection can be made as indicated.

The advocate may either allow the witness to tell his story in his own way, or he may bring out his testimony by a series of questions. If the witness is intelligent and honest, the best way is to let him tell his own story, but if he is stupid and inclined to speak of irrelevant matters, it is better to elicit his testimony by questions.

One rule that should never be violated is, that under all circumstances the advocate should keep cool, and not lose his temper. No matter how stupid the witness, or how unexpectedly damaging his testimony, or how exasperating the conduct of opposing counsel, or how erroneous he may think the rulings of the Court on questions of evidence, the advocate should show no more signs of discomposure than if he were a graven image. For aside from the fact that juries attach much importance to the effect of damaging testimony upon lawyers engaged in the trial of the case, if the advocate loses his temper he may say or do something fatal to his case, and to his reputation as an advocate. There are times when indignation should be expressed, but the advocate must keep within bounds, and deport himself with dignity, never forgetting the respect due the Court from himself as one of its officers, and never forgetting the respect due the office of advocate which his opponents hold as well as himself

If a witness is inclined to be pert or forward, the advocate should treat him gravely and distantly, and show him by his tone and manner that his levity or insolence is out of place in the Court-room, and that no trifling will be allowed.

If an advocate finds that a witness whom he has called is treacherous and unfriendly, there are two courses which he may pursue. One is not to appear to distrust him, and dismiss him as soon as possible, and the second is to open fire upon him and make him show his bias or prejudice. Both methods have their advantages and their disadvantages, and sometimes it is best to pursue one course and sometimes the other. Perhaps the former course is best if the witness is defiant, unscrupulous, and intelligent, the latter, if he is not naturally inclined to be combative. But it is better, if the advocate suspects that a witness may prove treacherous, to have a signed proof from him, signed if possible in the presence of reliable witnesses, with which to confront him in case it should prove necessary, and the Court should permit it (*vide ante*, pp. 31, note, and 35).

No question should be asked without a definite object in view. The time of the Court is taken up, the jury become weary and disgusted, when an advocate, merely for the purpose of showing himself wise or witty, spins out an examination to an unnecessary length. Besides, it is dangerous to ask questions which are aimless, for the answer of the witness is as likely to be unfavourable, as favourable. It is a safe rule not to ask a question unless the examiner has reason to believe the answer will be favourable.

No better general rules, for the examination of a witness in chief, that we know of, can be found, than those given by David Paul Brown, who was one of the greatest American advocates. His rules have stood the test of experience and have been found highly useful by the profession in the United States, and nearly every writer of note, on the subject, has borrowed largely from them. We feel that we could have no safer guide, and have concluded to give the rules in full ·—

DAVID PAUL BROWN'S GOLDEN RULES.

First. If your own witnesses are bold, and may injure your cause by pertness or forwardness, observe a ceremony and gravity of manner towards them which may be calculated to repress their assurance.

Second. If they are alarmed or diffident and their thoughts are evidently scattered, commence your examination with matters of a familiar character, remotely connected with the subject of their alarm, or the matter in issue, as for instance : " Where do you live ? " " Do you know the parties ? " " How long have you known them ? " and the like. When you have restored them to composure, and the mind has gained its equilibrium, proceed to the most essential features of the cause, being careful to be mild and distinct in your approaches, lest you may trouble the fountain again from which you are to drink

Third. If the evidence of your own witnesses be unfavourable to you—which should always be guarded against—exhibit no want of composure for there are many minds that form opinions of the nature or character of testimony chiefly from the effect which it may appear to produce upon the counsel.

Fourth If you see that the mind of the witness is imbued with prejudices against your client, hope but little from such a quarter—unless there be some facts which are essential to your client's protection, and which that witness alone can prove; either do not call him, or get rid of him as soon as possible If the opposite counsel see the bias to which I have referred he may employ it to your own ruin. In judicial inquiries, of all possible evils the worst and the hardest to resist is an enemy in the disguise of a friend. You cannot impeach him—you cannot disarm him—you cannot even indirectly assail him; and if you exercise the only privilege that is left to you, and call other witnesses for the purpose of an explanation, you must bear in mind that instead of carrying the war into the enemy's country, the struggle is between sections of your own forces, and in the very heart, perhaps, of your own camp. Avoid this by all means.

Fifth. Never call a witness whom your adversary will be compelled to call. This will afford you the privilege of cross-examination. Take from your opponent the small privilege it thus gives you, and, in addition thereto, not only render everything unfavourable said by the witness doubly operative against the party calling him, but also deprive that party of the power of counteracting the effect of the testimony.

Sixth. Never ask a question without an object—nor without being able to connect that object with the case, if objected to as irrelevant.

Seventh Be careful not to put your questions in such form that, if opposed for informality, you cannot sustain it, or at least produce strong reasons in its support. Frequent failures in the discussion of points of evidence enfeeble your strength in the estimation of the jury, and greatly impair your hopes in the final result.

Eighth. Never object to a question put by your adversary without being able and disposed to enforce the objection. Nothing is so monstrous as to be constantly making and withdrawing objections; it indicates either a want of correct perception in making them, or a deficiency of reason, or of moral courage in not making them good

Ninth. Speak to your witness clearly and distinctly, as if you were awake, and engaged in a matter of interest, and make him, also, speak distinctly and to your question. How can it be supposed that the Court and jury will be inclined to listen, when the only struggle seems to be whether the counsel or the witness shall first go to sleep?

Tenth. Modulate your voice as circumstances may direct. " Inspire the fearful and repress the bold."

Eleventh Never begin before you are ready, and always finish when you have done. In other words, do not question for question's sake—but for an answer.

* * * * *

Mr. Cox advises a different method of treatment of a party's adverse witnesses from that advised in the fourth " Golden Rule," given above. He says: " Make no secret of his enmity; on the contrary, you have most to dread when his manner and tone do not discover his feelings. If you are satisfied beyond doubt of his hostility, and he should, as is often seen, assume a frank and friendly mien in the witness-box, instead of accepting his approaches reject them with indignation, let him see that you are not to be imposed upon, and endeavour to provoke him to the exhibition of his true feelings."

It is difficult to decide which course is to be preferred where two such eminent authorities disagree, but we think that a middle course is to be chosen as a general rule. Perjury is not so common as it is thought to be by the inexperienced practitioner, and the tone of voice and manner of the advocate, while conducting the examination of witnesses, we think, is given undue prominence by the authors just mentioned, in all they say upon the subject of examination of witnesses. We are inclined to believe that a calm, courteous demeanour is best in all cases, and that the advocate should bear in mind that witnesses are entitled to more consideration than they sometimes receive at the hands of advocates who seem to think it their duty to bully or terrify them into telling the truth. Lord Coleridge, when at the bar, was considered a model examiner. He never lost his temper, and invariably treated all witnesses examined by him with the greatest courtesy, and by pursuing this course he obtained more favourable testimony than he would have obtained in any other way. Of course there are times when the advocate may safely depart from this general rule, but they are of comparatively rare occurrence.

The advocate should frame his questions with great care, in order that the witness may be enabled to readily understand him He should use the simplest language in which to express his ideas, and should call a spade a spade, and not an implement of husbandry. It is easy for an advocate to make a mistake of this kind. He is too apt to take it for granted that the witness is not only intelligent, but well educated.

The advocate should avoid asking leading questions where he can do so. While the general rule, which is well known, is that leading questions should not be asked, there are many exceptions to it, and the whole matter rests in the sound discretion of the Court. Leading questions may be asked upon matters which are not material but merely introductory or preliminary ; the

Court will permit them to be asked where the witness appears unwilling and hostile to the party calling him; they may be asked when they will assist the memory of a witness where it appears defective, especially if the subject is a complicated one; and lastly, they may be asked for the purpose of identifying persons or things, and the attention of the witness may be directly called to them.

Mr. Cox's advice as to the duties of opposing counsel pending examination in chief is so valuable that we shall give it entire. He says: "While the examination in chief is proceeding, it is the duty of the counsel on the other side to give the most attentive ear to every question and every answer, and to take a note of them. When this duty devolves upon you, it may, perhaps, be performed all the more satisfactorily by the observance of some rules which experience has approved.

"You must mark every question put to the witness, with a double purpose: first to be sure that it is properly put, according to the rules of evidence, and secondly, to ascertain what is its bearing upon the case, and the design of your adversary in putting it.

"Great keenness of perception and readiness of apprehension are requisite to the performance of this task. You will need to have the law of evidence at your fingers' ends, that if the question be an improper one, you may interpose instantly *before the answer is given*, to forbid the witness to reply, and then not only to make your objection to the Court, but to support it by *reasons*.

" And here let us warn you against the fault of making too frequent and too frivolous objections. Many inexperienced men appear to think, that by continually carping at the questions put by the other side to the witnesses, they are proving to the audience how clever they are. But this is a mistake. Such an exhibition of captiousness, whether affected or real, is offensive to the Court and to the jury. Nothing is more easy than to find opportunities for this sort of vanity, without starting objections actually untenable, because, in practice, a vast number of questions *are* put which in strictness are leading, and, therefore, if objected to, could not be permitted. But you should *never* object to a question, as leading, *merely because it is such*, but only when it appears to you to be likely to have an effect injurious to your cause. And when you have occasion to make such an objection, do it good-temperedly, and as appealing to the better judgment of your opponent, whether he does not deem it to be an improper question ; nor address the objection to the Court in the first instance but to your adversary, and only if he persists in putting it should you call upon the Court to decide between you which is right.

"But it is not only against improper leading questions you have to be upon the watch ; there are many others still more objectionable, which it will be your duty, by an instant objection, to prevent. As soon as the words have fallen from your opponent's lips, and before the witness can have time to answer, you must interpose, first, with an exclamation to the witness, 'Don't answer that,' and then, turning to the Court, state what is your objection to the question, with your reasons for it. Your opponent will answer you. Then you will have the right of replying, and the Court will decide between you !

"There is, perhaps, no part of the business of an advocate in which the fruits of experience are more obvious than in this. If you watch closely the examination of witnesses, in a trial where an experienced advocate is on the one side and an inexperienced one on the other, you will see the practised man putting question after question, and eliciting facts most damaging to the other side which his adversary might have shut out by a prompt objection to them, but which he permits to pass without protest, because he is not sufficiently practised in the law of evidence to discern their illegality on the instant, or so much master of it as to give a reason for objection, even though he may have a sort of dim sense that the questions are wrong somehow, and he protests against leading questions, while he permits illegal questions destructive to his client to be put without a murmur. On the other hand, when it comes his turn to examine his witnesses, and on the experienced man devolves the duty of watching, you will see how, in no single instance, is he suffered to tread over the traces ; but the strictest rules of evidence are enforced upon him, so that he sits down, leaving half his case undeveloped, while his adversary has brought out all that he desired to elicit.

" Hence to the student aspiring to be an advocate the vital importance of a mastery of the law of evidence, as the branch of law which is not only most frequently in requisition by him, but the only one which he is called upon to propound without previous research. Almost all other subjects are notified to him before he goes into Court, so that he may look into the law, and prepare himself for the argument ; or if, as rarely happens, he is suddenly called upon, the Court will always give him time for research, or, at the least, allowance is made for an insufficiency common to his audience, even to the Judge upon the bench. But in questions of evidence no such delay is practicable, and no such excuse is accepted. They necessarily arise on a sudden, and must be suddenly argued and decided. An advocate is expected to be aware of this, and to come prepared with a knowledge of all the principles and rules of evidence. In order to do this it is necessary to keep up his acquaintance with it, by continually refreshing his memory, not only by reading every day a portion of his favourite text-book, but by carefully reading, and then noting up in that text-book, which should be interleaved for that purpose, every case decided upon the law of evidence, as the reports issue ; and it is of the extremest importance that he should possess the very latest decisions, for they will not unfrequently give him a victory over an adversary not so well prepared as himself with the *latest cases.*

"While upon this subject it may be convenient to add that there is another class of cases of which an advocate should be careful to procure the earliest intelligence, and to note with equal care in his book of practice ; namely, such as may, perhaps, be best described under the collective title of 'The Practice of *Nisi Prius.'* We mean by this, cases equally in sudden requisition with those on evidence, as determining the conduct of a trial : as the right to begin, notices, juries, and verdicts, the measure of damages, exceptions. Many a victory has been won solely by the superior diligence of an advocate in thus possessing himself of the most recent decisions on cases of this class.

"Your notes of the evidence, as it proceeds, should be fully taken, because you cannot anticipate at this period of the cause what portion of it may prove to be material, nor where a question may arise as to what was the witness's answer. In taking these notes you begin with the day and date on which the trial took place, and the name of the Judge. You then, very briefly, note the more important points of the opening speech, especially such points as you purpose to answer, and you indicate such as will require peculiar attention by scoring them twice or thrice. Then stating the name of the witness and the counsel by whom he is examined, you set down his evidence, leaving a broad margin for your own observations, if any should occur to you. It is not necessary to give both question and answer, save where the question strikes you as one of special import, or to which you might desire thereafter to refer; it will suffice to give the answer in the witness's own words, as nearly as you can observe them, so as to make the statement intelligible. Thus, if the witness be asked, 'Were you at Exeter on Saturday?' and answers, 'I was,'—a leading

question, but probably not worth objecting to,—you set
it down thus: 'Was at Exeter on Saturday.' But let
it be a rule, so far as is practicable, always to take the
very words used by the witness. As you proceed, you
will find that the evidence suggests to you matter to be
explained on cross-examination, or to be answered in
your speech for the defence, or to be contradicted by
your own witness. Here it is that you will find the
margin useful. When such an idea occurs to you, never
suffer it to escape, trusting to recall it when it is wanted,
for, amid the multiplicity of claims upon your attention,
you cannot be assured that it will return; but grasp it
instantly, and in the margin, against the evidence that is
so to be treated, insert some mark which may catch your
eye, and if the words are not likely to suggest the thought
you desire to recall, you can, in a hurried sentence, there
set down that of which you wish to be reminded. This
plan is especially useful for the purpose of cross-examination, for it is extremely difficult to carry in the mind all
the evidence in chief that needs to be explained or
deprived of its credit; but with this scored and noted
report of the witness's testimony before you, it is unlikely
that anything of moment will escape your attention.

"Another duty may devolve upon you as advocate—
that is, the examination on the *voir dire*. This legal
phrase means merely the examination to which a witness
may be subjected before he is admitted to be sworn,
for the purpose of ascertaining if he is competent to be
a witness. When, therefore, a witness is called you must
be prepared, if you have an objection to him, to state it
immediately on his appearance and before he is sworn to
give his evidence between the parties, and having
intimated to the Court that you have such an objection,
you will proceed to examine him in support of it. This
examination you will be permitted to conduct as in the
nature of a cross-examination. Very few questions
usually suffice; but if you are dealing with an acute

witness, who knows your object, and especially with a professional one, no common skill and tact are often required to drag out of him the particular circumstances necessary to sustain your objection. The same rules apply to *voir dire* examinations as to cross-examinations."

    *   *   *   *   *

Many advocates have the happy faculty of cross-examining witnesses well, but the talent of conducting properly the examination in chief is extremely rare

The suggestions which we have made, we hope will be particularly serviceable to the young legal practitioner, but he can never expect to become expert until he has had great experience.

Mr Scarlett, as we have said, attached great importance to the examination in chief. He always, in important cases, after he became a leader, performed this duty himself, and from all accounts of the manner in which he performed this task, there have been very few advocates who have done it as well.

When conducting an examination in chief Mr. Scarlett showed very clearly by his countenance that he believed there was no more truthful person in the world than his witness under examination

An interesting account of Scarlett's manner in Court is given by one of his contemporaries. This account was written while Mr. Scarlett was alive, and is, we think, calculated to give a clear insight into his manner, casting a spell over Court, jury and witnesses .—

"He waits patiently to detect that weak point, in respect of technical learning, which his adversary is almost sure to manifest; and then, with the confidence and self-possession of an accomplished pleader, fixes upon that for the front of his own battle; and with his hands tucked under his silk gown behind him, and that look of conciliating good-fellowship with which Mr. Scarlett has, somehow or other, a trick of persuading the Judges and

securing the jury, he rarely fails to defeat the formidable
array of his antagonist, and to gain his own point at the
expense only of a few smiles and a little display of able
pleading. There is something very skilful in the position
that Mr. Scarlett invariably assumes while addressing
the Court where the disposition of the court-house will
allow of it. He is fond of giving to the jury that sort
of view of his own countenance which best enables him
to read the expression of theirs ; and no man ever knew
mo e astutely how to assume, as if by involuntary emotion,
the contracting frowns of doubt or the dilating aspect
of conviction as a witness under examination happens
to be deposing for or against his case, or as the charge
of the Judge refers particular points to the discretion
of the jury, their judgment upon which Mr. Scarlett
has the usual honest desire of an advocate to influence.
The jury, I have thought more than once, are rather
captivated by the sleek, English-like open face of Mr.
Scarlett ; and the shades of opinion which seem to pass
over it have at least as much power over the judgments
of most jurors as the more intellectual distinctions and
principles that are elaborately defined to them by his
lordship.

" His chief talents lie in a prompt and almost intuitive
discernment of the best features of the case before him,
and as ready a power to render them obvious to the com-
monest members of a common jury. Leaving points of
law and pleadings upon them to junior counsel, who have
more time to search for authorities, and get together the
arguments they suggest, Mr. Scarlett mostly directs his
attention to that persuasive influence and effect, which
the speeches of a masterly advocate seldom fail to
exercise over the minds of ordinary men, appointed to
determine, not the law, but the facts of the case before
them.

" In this task no man of the present day has been
more uniformly successful. Without superior genius,

and with no lofty or vivid imagination, Mr. Scarlett has managed, by a fine command of language and of voice, and a judicious selection and compression of the best arguments, to arrest attention and implant conviction with surprising effect. In the opposite talent, too, of making things difficult of comprehension, of involving them in the mazes of subtlety and covering them with the shroud of darkness, when the cause of his client requires it, this individual is as expert as the most ingenious of his fellows, and far more so than the shrewdest of those to whom he has generally been opposed.

"While Mr. Brougham opposes to him an overwhelming accumulation of the intelligence, analogies, authorities; and grapples with his argument in the strength of his wonderful ingenuity, his great acuteness, and his sarcastic and unsparing ridicule; how does the other meet such a fearful display of intellect and energy?"

The following are the rules given by Mr. Cox for conducting the examination in chief:—

"The plaintiff's case being thus stated by the leader, the examination of the plaintiff's witnesses proceeds. The general rule is for the counsel on that side to conduct the examination of the witnesses in turn, the junior taking the first witness, probably because it was supposed that the leader would require rest after his speech. But this order is sometimes departed from under special circumstances—as where the witness is peculiarly important, or his examination demands peculiar skill—in which case the leader will propose to take him, a suggestion to which you should always readily and cheerfully assent; and, indeed, when such a witness chances to fall to your lot, it would be becoming in you to propose to your leader that he should call him, and thus to anticipate the delicacy that often prevents a leader from doing that which may look like a want of confidence in you.

"An impression very generally prevails in both

branches of the profession, that the examination in chief
is an easy task, which anybody may perform, and demanding neither ability nor experience. But this is a
grave mistake, and the difficulty of the one as of the
other will be discovered at the first experiment. You
probably suppose that you have nothing to do but to take
your brief in your hand and carry your witness through
his evidence, as it is there set down, turning aside neither
to the right hand nor to the left, and, when you have
come to the end of the statement on the paper, to
resume your seat and leave him to be dealt with by
your adversary in cross-examination. But your task is
far from being so easy, for, in the first place, you cannot
always rely upon the evidence as stated in the brief.
The attorney does not always know what is and what is
not admissible evidence, and, if he has a doubt, he
prudently states rather than omit it, deeming that it may
be useful to you for information, although you cannot
bring it directly before the Court. The witnesses themselves cannot always be relied upon in their statements
made to the attorney, and upon which the brief is
framed. Nothing is more common than to find assertions, most confidently made in the office, retracted in
the witness-box, under the sanction of an oath and the
fear of cross-examination. Witnesses have so many
motives for *stretching* their stories to the attorney—the
love of being important, the desire to be taken to the
assizes and paid for pleasure trips—that it is often
impossible by any vigilance to keep them to the strict
literal truth in their statements given in the office, and
unless you are prepared for this kind of disappointment
in your examination in chief, you will be sorely disconcerted and put to confusion. And here let us warn you
against the danger which inexperience frequently incurs,
of being not only disconcerted by the witness failing to
support his previous statements, but by exhibiting in
countenance or manner the disappointment you feel.

Let nothing—not even a tone of your voice—betray surprise, or it will assuredly reveal your weakness to your lynx-eyed opponent, who may make use of the fact to discredit your witness and your cause, by the argument, always powerful, that the witness has told two different stories. And hence the necessity for another rule of examination, *to make as little use as possible of your brief*. You should commit to memory the leading facts to be proved by the witness, or note them in the margin in such a manner that, *as the brief lies upon the table*, your eye may catch in an instant anything you may have forgotten as you go along; but do not hold the brief before you like a book from which you are reading, as you will inevitably examine the witness as if you were hearing him repeat a catechism he has learned, instead of gathering from him information which *he* possesses but you do *not*. Have a synopsis of the leading facts before you. If you read your questions from your brief, you will find it very difficult, whatever the necessity, to depart from the terms or the order there set down. But if you examine from your memory, or such an outline of the facts as we have suggested, your brief lying upon the table, your whole attention will be given to the witness, your eye to his deportment, your mind to his words, and knowing what you want to have from him, you will be enabled to adapt your questions in accordance with what has preceded, and so as to procure the facts you are seeking. It happens frequently that new facts come out in examination, which materially alter the complexion of the case, and require a complete remodelling of the entire train of questions, with a view to elicit explanation, and to make the whole consistent with your case. Such a position will demand the exercise of all your ingenuity and caution, and it is in such a position that the skill of the accomplished advocate is discovered, far more than in those oratorical displays which win for him the applause of the public. The attorney and the counsel in a cause alone know the real and greatest merits of an advocate.

" You are, of course, acquainted with the first great rule of practice in the examination in chief, that you shall not put leading questions to your own witness, a leading question being such a one as suggests the answer. This rule is simple, and seemingly easy of application, but you will find it to be excessively difficult to be observed in practice, and, indeed, if it were strictly enforced, a trial would be prolonged indefinitely. At the beginning of your practice, having this rule continually ringing in your ears, from the interruptions of unpractised juriors trying to appear very clever and very quick, you will be apt to err rather by its too strict observance, than by violating it. Nevertheless, as it is often enforced without necessity, merely for the sake of interruption, you must be prepared to cope with its difficulties, and we will endeavour to point out the most prominent of them.

"But first observe that the rule against leading questions is properly applicable *only to such questions as relate to the matter at issue.* Whatever some priggish opponent may suggest, it is permitted to you—and the Judge will encourage you in the practice—to lead the witness directly up to the point at issue. It saves time and clears the case, and if you narrowly observe experienced advocates, you will find that they always adopt this course. For instance, instead of putting the introductory questions, 'Where do you live?' 'What are you?' and so forth, you should, unless there be some special reason to the contrary, directly put the leading questions, 'Are you a banker, carrying on business in Lombard Street?' and so on, until you approach the questionable matter, when, of course, you will proceed to conduct the examination according to the strict rule.

" But that rule is not so easily to be observed as you may suppose. Frequently it will occur that you will have need to call the attention of the witness to something he may have forgotten—as thus · Suppose that you were examining as to a certain conversation. The witness has narrated the greater portion of it, but he has omitted a passage which is of importance to you. We know that, in fact, with all of us, in our calmest moments, it is difficult to repeat perfectly the whole of what was said at a certain interview, and if it had been a long one probably we might repeat it half-a-dozen times, and each time omit a different portion of it, although in either case the omitted part would be instantly recalled to our memories if we were asked, 'Did he not also say so-and-so?' or, 'Was not something said about so-and-so?' But this sort of reminiscent question you are not permitted to put to a witness, because it would be a leading question, although he is far more likely, in his agitation, to forget that he had not repeated the whole than we should be in our calmest moments In vain you ask him, 'Did anything more pass between you?' 'Was nothing more said?' 'Have you stated all that occurred?' He does not in fact remember precisely what he has stated of it, or the portion you desire to obtain has escaped his memory for the moment. It would flash upon him instantly if it were to be repeated, or even to be half uttered. But you may not help him so, and then there arises a perplexity which every advocate must often have experienced—in what manner can this be recalled without leading? Here is another occasion for the exercise of that ready tact in the conduct of an examination in chief which marks the skilful advocate. Your endeavour must now be to suggest indirectly the forgotten statement, and to do so without violating the rule, which in this respect is certainly pushed further than justice and fairness to the infirmity of human memory can sanction. As each case must depend upon its circumstances, it is impossible to lay down any rule to help you, or even to hint at forms of suggestion. But one method we may name, as having proved efficacious when

others have failed, and that is, to make the witness repeat
his account of the interview, or whatever it may be, then
it will not unfrequently happen, as we have already
observed, that he will remember and repeat the passage
you require, and omit something else which he had
previously stated. But this, of course, matters not; your
object has been gained, and your adversary may take
what advantage he can of the difference in the statements
If the story is a long one, you will avoid inflicting this
repetition of it until other expedients have been tried in
vain. It may be added, that a single word often suffices
to suggest the whole sentence, if you have a quick wit,
you may sometimes bring out the matter you want by so
framing a question that it shall contain a part of the
forgotten sentence *ipsissimis verbis*, but otherwise
applied.

"Great caution is required in the examination of all
your witnesses, after the first, to prevent their disagree-
ment in any important particulars. No error of
inexperience or unskilfulness is more common than
to examine a witness according to the brief, without
reference to the evidence previously given and the
requirements of the case as it stands. If you fear that
there may be conflicting testimony on any point, the
first witness having varied from the statement in the
brief, it is usually better to leave it as it stands upon
that single testimony than to bring out a contradiction;
but upon this you must exercise your sagacity at the
moment; it must depend upon the particular facts of
the case. We only suggest to you that it is one of the
difficulties of examination in chief which you should be
prepared to encounter. Anticipating it, you will not be
taken by surprise when it occurs to you in your practice.

"There are two kinds of troublesome witnesses whom
you will have to encounter in the conduct of a cause—
those who say too much, and those who say too little;
your too eager friends and your secret enemies. Of

these, by far the most difficult to deal with are your over-zealous friends—your witnesses who *prove too much*. A very little experience will enable you to detect these personages almost at a glance, certainly after a few sentences. They usually try to look wonderfully easy and confident, answer off-hand with extraordinary glibness, and give you twice as much information as you have asked for. Now, another rule of evidence is, that *you shall not discredit your own witnesses*, so that your only chance of dealing with these troublesome friends is to check them at the very outset, by kindly but gravely and peremptorily requiring them to do no more than simply to answer the questions you may put to them, and then so to frame your questions that the answer to them shall be a plain 'yes' or 'no,' giving them no opportunity for expatiating. Keep them closely to the point for which they are required, and having got from them just what you want, dismiss them, right thankful if they have not done you more harm than good. Witnesses of the character just described often do more harm than good to the party calling them.

"There is no more difficult and delicate task, in the conduct of an examination in chief, than so skilfully to manage an adverse witness called by yourself, that he shall state just so much as you require and no more.

"When the Court is satisfied that the witness is really an adverse one, the strict rule which forbids leading questions will be relaxed, and you will be permitted to conduct the examination somewhat more after the manner of a cross-examination. But this is only a partial licence. You may put leading questions, but you may not discredit him, whatever may have been the damage done to you by his testimony, and however obvious the *animus* which has misrepresented the facts purposely for the injury of your cause. He is still *your* witness, and having chosen to call him, and thereby to ask the jury to believe his story, it is not competent to you to turn round when you find he does not suit your purpose, and endeavour to show to the jury that he is unworthy of credit. Between this Scylla and Charybdis lies your difficult course in dealing with such a witness

"As a general rule, the less you say to such a witness the better for you. Bring him directly to the point which he is called to prove, frame your questions so that they shall afford the least possible room for evasion, or, what is still worse, *explanation*. Avail yourself of your liberty to lead as soon as you can—that is, as soon as you have laid the foundation for it by showing from his manner that the witness is really averse. You should not conceal your knowledge of the fact that the witness is hostile. Provoke him, when he attempts to appear friendly, to an exhibition of hostility in order to show that he is an enemy in the guise of a friend. By pursuing this course you will prevent the witness from imposing upon you, and will expose his treachery and perfidy to the Court and jury. The importance of so doing will be obvious to you when you remember that it is essential to the safety of your cause that the jury should receive his testimony with a knowledge of the circumstances under which it is given, so that anything adverse to you which may fall from him shall be accepted by them with the allowance which is always made by reasonable men for the exaggerations or even inventions of an enemy; for, to an audience so prepared, whatever falls from him in your favour will have double value given to it, and whatever he may say that tells against you will be rejected. Hence it is the first care of a skilful advocate, in dealing with his own adverse witness, not only *not to conceal* the hostility, but to make it prominent—to provoke it to an open display, and draw out the expression of the feeling, if it does not sufficiently appear without a stimulus. If he be adverse at all, *you cannot make him appear too adverse*, because the more hostile he is, the more will his evidence in your favour be esteemed, and the less weight will be given to such as he may utter against you. [If possible, the cause of the enmity of the witness should be shown out of his own mouth. The relation of the witness to opposite party should also be carefully inquired into If he is adverse, a skilful examination will lay bare his motive.]

" If your witness be timid, it will be your care to restore his self-possession before you take him to the material part of his testimony This you should effect by assuming a cheerful and friendly manner and tone, and if you have the art to make him smile, your wit would be better timed than is always the case with forensic jests. Keep him thus employed upon the fringe of the case, until you are satisfied that his courage is restored, and then you may proceed with him as with any other witness But be very careful not to take him to material topics while he is under the influence of fear, for in this state a witness is apt to become confused, and to contradict himself, and so to afford to your adversary a theme for damaging comment. [The reader is requested to compare this rule with the second golden rule of David Paul Brown, already given.]

" A *stupid* witness is often more troublesome than an adverse one. He cannot understand your questions, or answers them so imperfectly that he had better left them unanswered. With such a one the only resource is patience and good temper. If you are cross with him you will be sure to increase his stupidity, and to convert evidence that means nothing into evidence that is contradictory and confused The preservation of imperturbable good temper is a golden rule with an advocate. He should never be moved to anger by anything, however provoking, and however he may appear to be in a passion. Entire self-command is his greatest virtue, never more in requisition than in dealing with a stupid witness. Instead of rebuking him, you should encourage him by a look and expression of approval, and you must frame your question in another shape better suited to his dense faculties. If baffled again, do not retreat, but renew the catechism until your object is obtained. In constructing your questions, you will often find a clue to his train of thought by observing his answers, and your next question might then, with a little ingenuity, be so framed as to fall in with his train of ideas. Thus patiently treated, there are few witnesses so dull as not to be made efficient for the purpose of an examination in chief.

"In this, as in opening your case to the jury, it is the better course to observe the order of *time*. That is not only the most easily intelligible to the jury, but it is the natural order in which events are associated in the mind of the witness, and therefore by which they are the most readily and accurately recalled. If you depart from this for the sake of bringing facts that are connected together by some other link than time, as, for instance, to exhibit in its entirety one branch of your case, let the same principle govern the order of that, and then return to the original plan. But it will not do to revert to the precise point where you quitted it, you should repeat the two or three questions with which you concluded, so as to recall your witness to the point from which you have diverted him. Inattention to this simple rule is often the occasion of no small perplexity to the witness, and it is scarcely necessary to warn you against that of which advantage is certain to be taken to damage your case.

"Your manner in examination in chief should be very different from that which you assume in cross-examination. You are dealing with your own witness, whom you assume to be friendly to you, unless informed to the contrary, when it is permitted to you to take the tone already described. You must encourage him if he be timid, and win his confidence by a look and voice of friendliness. It often happens that witnesses, unaccustomed to Courts of justice, are so alarmed at their own new position, that in their confusion they cannot at first distinguish between the friendly and the adverse counsel, and they treat you as an enemy to be kept at bay, and to whom they are to impart as little as possible. It is then your care to set your witness right, and a kindly smile will often succeed in doing this. Do not appear to notice his embarrassment, for that is sure to increase it, but remove it quietly and imperceptibly by pleasant looks, friendly tones, and words that have not the stern sound of a catechism, but the familiar request of a companion to impart a story which the querist is anxious to hear and the other gratified to tell The most frightened witness may thus be drawn almost unconsciously into a narrative which, when he entered the witness-box, had escaped his memory in his terror.

" Your questions in examination in chief should be framed carefully, and put deliberately. You never require in this that rapid fire of questions which, as we shall have occasion to show hereafter, is so often requisite in cross-examination Nor in this have you need to put an immaterial question, save under the rare circumstances previously described. You should weigh every question in your mind before you put it, in order that it may be so framed as to bring out in answer just so much as you desire, and no more. You have time for this, if you are as quick of thought as an advocate should be, while the Judge is taking his note of the previous answer ; but even if this be not sufficient for your purpose, you must not fear to make a deliberate pause. The Court will soon learn not to be impatient of your seeming slowness, when it discovers that you have in fact abbreviated the work by a pause which has enabled you to keep the evidence strictly to the point at issue.

" They who remember Sir William Follett will at once understand our meaning, for one of his most remarkable and impressive peculiarities was the grave and thoughtful

deliberation with which he framed and put his questions to his own witnesses, and the result of which was
that he was seldom annoyed by unexpected answers or
by additions and explanations which he did not desire.

"Sometimes it demands considerable discretion to
determine whether it is better to permit the witness to
tell his own story in his own way, or to take him through
it by questions. No rule can be laid down for this; it
must depend upon your discernment at the moment.
There is a class of minds which can only recall facts
by recalling all the associated circumstances, however
irrelevant; they must repeat the whole of a long
dialogue, and describe the most trivial occurrences of the
time, in order to arrive at any particular part of the
transaction. With such you have no help for it but to
let them have their own way. It is the result of a
peculiar mental constitution, and endeavours to disturb
their trains of association will only produce inextricable
confusion in the ideas of the witnesses, and you will be
further than ever from arriving at your object. But if
you are dealing with that other class of witnesses,
happily more rare, who appear to have no trains of
thought at all, who can observe no order of events, whose
ideas are confused as to time, place, and person, your
only chance of extracting anything to your purpose is to
begin by requesting that they will simply answer your
questions, and falling in, as it were, with their own
mental condition, proceed to interrogate them, after
their own fashion, with disconnected questions, and so
endeavour to draw out of them isolated facts, which
you will afterward connect together in your reply, or
which may dovetail with the rest of the evidence, so as
to form a complete story.

"This plan will often be found effective with such
witnesses, when all 'he usual methods of eliciting a
narrative from them have been abandoned in despair.
Of course it demands great tact and readiness; but it is

presumed that unless you possess these qualities you will not attempt to become an advocate.

"It is, perhaps, almost an impertinence to tell you that you are by no means bound to call the witnesses in the order in which they are placed in the brief.

"It will be your task, when reading and noting up your case, to marshal your witnesses in the order in which they will best support your case, as you have determined to submit it to the jury. But, inasmuch as you are not permitted to recall your witnesses except with special permission of the Court, given only under special circumstances, and you are therefore compelled to elicit all that you require in order to support any part of your case, where the same witness speaks to different parts of it, you must take care in his examination to separate his testimony as it relates to each of such parts, and even at the expense of some repetition to take him through his evidence as it bears upon one part before you take him to another, observing, however, the rules as to time and the manner of reverting to the former portion of the narrative, which have been previously described."

CHAPTER III.

CROSS-EXAMINATION.

BEFORE making suggestions as to the manner in which the cross-examination should be conducted, we will give a few of the leading principles of the law of evidence which should govern counsel in the conduct of the cross-examination.

Cross-examination undoubtedly affords the best security against incomplete, distorted, or false evidence, and in putting questions upon cross-examination, much greater latitude in asking questions is allowed than upon examination in chief. Especially is this true where the object of the questions asked is to affect the credit of the witness, and questions of this kind have been allowed where they affected the character of the witness and consequently his credit, although such questions had no relation to the matters in issue.

A witness, however, cannot be cross-examined as to any facts which, if admitted, would be collateral and wholly irrelevant to the matters in issue, and which could in no manner affect his credit. (*Cf. ante*, pp. 23, 24, and notes.)

Witnesses upon cross-examination may be asked as to any vindictive or revengeful expressions they may have used against any party to the cause, where such expressions would affect the credit or the character of the witness. But the answers of witnesses to irrelevant questions cannot, as a general rule, be contradicted; consequently, if a party choose to cross-examine a witness as to an irrelevant and collateral fact, he is bound by the answer of the witness. *Spenceley* v. *Willett*, 7 East, 109; *Harris* v. *Tippett*, 2 Camp. 637.

It is well settled that a witness may be asked if upon some former occasion a different and contradictory account of the same subject was given. If the witness gives an affirmative answer, the question affects his credit, of course, whether the subject of the answer be relevant or irrelevant to the issues involved. If, however, he answers in the negative *and the subject of the answer be irrelevant to the issues*, the answer is conclusive and the witness cannot be contradicted by other witnesses. But if the subject of the answer be relevant to the issues, then evidence may be given to show that on a former occasion the witness has given a different account of the same subject, and the inquiry is made for the purpose of laying a foundation for proof of contradictory statements.*

There are two exceptions to the rule that if a witness is cross-examined as to facts not material to the issue betw.. n the parties, his answer must be taken, and may not be contradicted.

(i.) Convictions for felony and misdemeanour, if denied, may be proved under the Crim. Proc. Act, 1865, ss. 1, 6; see p. 23, note. †

(ii.) If a witness deny on cross-examination having made statements which impeach his impartiality and therefore his credibility, evidence may be called to prove that he did make such statements. *R.* v. *Yewing*, 2 Camp. 638. Evidence of bribery of a witness, or subornation, though denied by the witness, may for similar reasons be given. *Att.-Gen.* v. *Hitchcock*, 1 Exch. 93; *R.* v. *Hitchcock*, 7 How. St. Tr. 446.

The contradictory statements to which we have referred may be of two kinds, verbal or in writing.

---

* *Cf. ante*, pp. 23, 24. This course may even be adopted in the examination in chief of the party's own witness, provided that the witness is, in the opinion of the Judge, hostile, and that the Judge's permission has been first obtained; *ante*, pp. 31 note, 35

† In criminal cases, where the prisoner is called as a witness the prosecution may not ask any question tending to show that the prisoner has been previously convicted or is of bad character, except in the cases mentioned in the Act (*vide* p. 170, *post*)

Where an inquiry is to be made touching contradictory verbal statements, the law is now settled by the Crim. Proc. Act, 1865, "Mr. Denman's Act," ss. 1, 4, the effect of which is that the witness must be asked upon cross-examination, all the particulars as to the supposed contradictions which are to be afterwards brought forward against him, before any contradiction is attempted, and he must be also asked as to the time, place and person involved in the supposed contradiction.

The reason of this rule is found in justice, and is intended to protect the witness, for as the direct tendency of the evidence is to impeach his veracity, by showing that he has made a contradictory statement to someone else, justice requires that, before his credit is attacked, he should have an opportunity to state whether he made such statement to that person, and of explaining, in the re-examination, the nature and particulars of the conversation, under what circumstances it was made, from what motives and with what design. It is a matter of common knowledge that it is very easy to be mistaken as to what was said in conversation. It may have been only partially heard, or partially forgotten, and besides, it may have been falsely reported; consequently, where the difference between his present statement which he makes upon oath, and the former statement as reported by a third person, may be as much owing to the mistake of the one witness as the misrepresentation of the other, it is but just that the memory of both witnesses should be fairly tried and contrasted.

It was formerly a matter of some doubt whether a verbal statement of the character we have mentioned can be proved where a witness has been asked about it, and he neither admits nor denies it. But the Crim. Proc. Act, 1865, ss. 1, 4, has now settled the matter, the words of s. 4 being, " If a witness . . . does not distinctly admit that he has made such statement, proof may be given that he did in fact make it."

The cross-examination of a witness as to previous statements in writing and the contradiction of a witness by means of such a writing are matters now dealt with by statute.

Criminal Procedure Act, 1865, ss 1, 5, provides that " a witness may be cross-examined as to previous statements made by him in writing, or reduced into iting, relative to the subject-matter of the indictment proceeding, without such writing being shown to him ; but if it is intended to contradict such witness by the writing, his attention must, before such contradictory proof can be given, be called to those parts of the writing which are to be used for the purpose of contradicting him ; provided always that it shall be competent for the Judge, at any time during the trial, to require the production of the writing for his inspection, and he may thereupon make such use of it for the purposes of the trial as he shall think fit."

The question was much discussed in the *Queen's Case*, 2 B. & B. 287, in the House of Lords, and in the case of the witness Louisa Dumont (Print Ev. 328, 334) the following question was put to the Judges for their opinion : " Whether a party on cross-examination would be allowed to represent, in the statement of a question, the contents of a letter, and to ask the witness whether the witness wrote a letter to any person with such contents, or contents to the like effect, without having first shown to the witness the letter, and having asked the witness whether he wrote that letter, and his admitting that he wrote such letter." The Judges were of the opinion that the question must be answered in the negative, and the reasons given for their opinion, as delivered by Abbott, C.J, were that " the contents of every written paper are, according to the ordinary and well-established rules of evidence, to be proved by the paper itself, and by that alone, if the paper be in existence. The proper course, therefore, is to ask the witness

whether or no that letter is of the handwriting of the
witness; if the witness admits that it is of his handwriting, the cross-examining counsel may, at the proper
season, read that letter as evidence; and when the letter
is produced, then the whole of the letter is made evidence. One of the reasons of the rule requiring the
production of written instruments is, in order that the
Court may be possessed of the whole. If the course
which is here proposed should be followed, the cross-
examining counsel may put the Court in possession only
of a part of the contents of the written paper; and thus
the Court may never be in possession of the whole,
though it may happen that the whole, if produced,
might have an effect very different from that which
might be produced by the statement of a part."

But now, under the section just referred to, counsel
may *cross-examine* a witness as to the contents of a
letter without showing it to him. The cross-examining
counsel may also when it is produced, if he desires, show
the witness only a part, or only one or more lines of the
letter, and not the whole of it, and may ask him whether
he wrote such part, or such one or more lines. But if the
witness does not admit that he wrote the letter, or the
part shown to him, he cannot be cross-examined as to
the contents of the letter for the reasons given, namely,
that the paper itself ought to be produced, in order that
the whole may be seen and the one part explained by
the other. If the witness, however, admits that he wrote
the letter, still the rule respecting cross-examination as
to contents is precisely the same, and the counsel cannot
ask whether such statements are in the letter; the letter
itself must be read in order to see whether it contains
such statement. As to the time for reading such letter, the
ordinary rule is, that it shall be read as the evidence of
the counsel cross-examining, as part of his evidence, in
his turn after he shall have opened his case; but if he suggests to the Court that he wishes to have the letter read

immediately in order to found certain questions upon the contents, which cannot well or effectually be done without reading the letter itself, in that case, for the sake of convenience, the letter is permitted to be read at the suggestion of the counsel; still, however, it must be considered as part of the evidence of the cross-examining counsel.

To sum up the state of the law in England to-day on this point :—A distinction must be made between the use that counsel may make of a writing in cross-examination (i.) without having to put the writing into the witness's hands, (ii) without having to put the writing in as evidence.

As to (i) he may ask a witness (a) whether he wrote a certain letter (without referring to its contents).

(b) He may go further and cross-examine as to its contents, or part only of its contents, without showing the writing to the witness.

But he may not contradict the witness's answers by putting the letter in evidence, until he has shown the letter to the witness, and given him an opportunity of explaining.

As to (ii.), he may ask a witness (a) whether he has written a certain document (which may or may not be shown to the witness, *vide supra*), or

(b) he may hand the document to the witness, and having asked him whether he wrote it, he may put his client's view of the facts to the witness, and ask him whether, having read the letter, he persists in his former evidence (*Birchall* v. *Bullough* (1896), 1 Q. B. 325), without having to put in the writing as evidence (unless the Judge requires him to do so under the proviso to s. 5 of the Crim. Proc. Act)

But he may not put the contents of the writing, *as such*, to the witness, and cross-examine him upon the writing, without putting the whole of the writing in as evidence.

Case (ii.) (b), in skilful hands, may prove a very useful form of procedure.

Thus, to take a concrete instance, you may, as counsel,

be in possession of a letter, written by the witness, in which he has made a statement at variance with his present testimony But the statement, though in this one particular in your favour, may be otherwise extremely hostile to your case. And you would thus be confined to such use of the letter as you could make of it, without having to put the whole letter in evidence

In this case, you would ask the witness whether he wrote such a letter, and then handing it to him, and allowing him to read it to himself, you would ask him *not* whether he had written something there which did not tally with his present testimony, but whether, having read the letter, he persisted in the statement made in his testimony that day And, in the case of an honest witness, the result might very well be that he would qualify that statement in your favour

And your opponent would not by this means become entitled to see the document you were using, *nor* to re-examine upon it, though of course he may re-examine upon the subject-matter of your questions.

It is well settled that a witness cannot be compelled to criminate himself in answer to a question But the witness may be compelled to answer if the offence is barred by the statute of limitations, or if he has been pardoned (*cf.* p 22, *ante*).

Sir James Scarlett once said of Mr. Topping, an eminent leader on the same circuit, that his idea of cross-examination was putting over again every question asked in chief in a very angry tone , and this is a fault from which members of the bar to-day are not always free.

It is highly important, in cross-examination, for the advocate to frame his questions in plain, simple language, adapted to the understanding of the witness. It often occurs, in the course of the examination of witnesses, that the witness does not understand the questions of the examiner, and the examiner does not understand the answers of the witness. A provincial pronunciation of words is a source of mistakes of this kind. A few examples will serve to make our meaning plain.

On Boswell telling Dr. Johnson of an earthquake which had been felt in Staffordshire, Dr. Johnson said to him: "Sir, it will be much exaggerated in public talk; for in the first place, the common people do not accurately adapt their words to their faults, they do not mean to lie; but taking no pains to be exact, they give you very false accounts A great part of their language is proverbial. If anything rocks at all, they say *it rocks like a cradle;* and in this way they go on."

"Clearness," says Wesley to one of his lay-assistants, "is necessary for you and me, because we are to instruct people of the lowest understanding; therefore, we, above all, if we *think* with the wise, must yet *speak* with the vulgar. We should constantly use the most common, little, easy words (so they are pure and proper) which our language affords. When first I talked at Oxford to plain people in the castle or the town, I observed they gaped and stared. This quickly obliged me to alter my style, and adopt the language of those I spoke to."

Sir Walter Scott, in "The Bride of Lammermoor," gives an amusing instance in point: "The blade-bone of a shoulder of mutton is called in Scotland a 'poor man,' as in some parts of England it is termed a 'poor Knight of Windsor', in contrast, it must be presumed, to the baronial Sir Loin. It is said that in the last age an old Scottish peer, whose conditions (none of the most gentle) were marked by a strange and fierce-looking exaggeration of the Highland countenance, chanced to be indisposed while he was in London attending Parliament. The master of the hotel where he lodged, anxious to show attention to his noble guest, waited on him to enumerate the contents of his well-stocked larder, so as to endeavour to hit on something which might suit his appetite. 'I think, landlord,' said his lordship, rising up from his couch, and throwing back the tartan plaid, with which he had screened his grim and ferocious visage, —'I think I could eat a morsel of a "*poor man*."' The landlord fled in terror, having no doubt that his guest was a cannibal who might be in the habit of eating a slice of a tenant, as light food, when he was under regimen."

It is said that Lord Eldon, when examined for a scholarship, in answer to the questions usual on such occasions, stated his father was a "fitter" (factor), and he so pronounced the word as to be mistaken for "fiddler." On the close of the examination, the President of the Board of Examiners said, "There is no doubt young Scott is by far the best scholar, but he has told us his father is a fiddler, and I do not quite like to take the son of a fiddler into the college."

It will readily be seen from these illustrations that great attention should be given to this matter. Rufus Choate and Daniel Webster were partial to plain, simple words.

Many advocates who use words of "learned length and thundering sound" in their questions to witnesses would do well to adopt a more homely and less truculent style.

Witnesses feel more at home when questioned in this way, and the jury will understand what is said as well as the Court and opposing counsel, for men never become so learned that they cannot understand simple language better than any other.

At the outset we wish to emphasise the advantage to be gained by treating hostile witnesses kindly, except in rare cases. A writer of experience says upon this point. "Docility and friendliness of a witness are of the utmost consequence. And courtesy toward him is a probable means to obtain and keep him, courtesy in words, voice and manner. Rudeness and incivility toward him is very likely to put him out of temper, and to make him lay back his ears.

" Little peculiarities of his nature must be humoured ; his sense of personal dignity must not be offended; if he be deaf, or have an impediment in his speech, this infirmity must not be a subject of merriment ; and if his voice be naturally or from timidity low, he should be gently, not roughly, exhorted to speak up. So, if the witness exhibit any clownish or awkward habit or manner, it may be better to let it pass unnoticed than to attempt to correct it.

" It is a common practice to tell a witness over and over again to mind he is upon his oath. Few witnesses bear this repeated admonition patiently. But when used in moderation and free from angry tone, the witness has no reason to complain of it, for it is known that some persons will *say* what they will not *swear*."

Courts and juries appreciate delicacy of feeling upon the part of advocates, and where in cross-examination it becomes important to inquire into the past history of a witness, or to speak about the death of a near relative or dear friend, or to touch some chord of sorrow, it is wise to use introductory expressions deploring the necessity of asking such questions, and representing it as one of the unpleasant but imperative duties of counsel is proper. Cicero furnishes an instance of this consideration for the feelings of others in his own person, in his defence of Cluentius, one of the charges against whom was that of having poisoned a son of one of the witnesses. Referring to this charge, he says :—" I deny that this young man, who you say died immediately after drinking from the cup, died on that day at all. It is a great and impudent falsehood. Look at the facts. I say that he came to the dinner unwell, and, with the imprudence of youth, indulged too much at it , that he was ill for some days after, and so died. Who is the witness that speaks to this ? he who mourns for his death,—his father; his father, I say, who, from his parental distress, would rise from the place where he is sitting to witness against

Cluentius if he had the slightest suspicion of his guilt; he by his testimony acquits him. But " (addressing the father) "stand up, I pray, a moment, while, however painful it may be, you repeat this necessary evidence, in the course of which I will not detain you long; you have ᵒted most righteously in not suffering your sorrow to ᵣavour a false charge against a man who is innocent."

Jurors are apt to sympathise with a witness who is unjustly attacked by counsel upon cross-examination, and in making up their verdict are often unconsciously influenced by such improper conduct upon the part of advocates. It is in vain that we deplore the fact that jurors are often influenced by passion or prejudice, and that they do not always follow the strict letter of the law, but, generally speaking, they mean to do what is right, and if they sometimes lean a little too far to the side of mercy, who can blame them?

The observations of Archbishop Whately, on the unfair treatment of witnesses by counsel, are worthy of consideration In this connection he says : " I think that the kind of skill by which the cross-examiner succeeds in alarming, misleading or bewildering an honest witness may be characterised as the most, or one of the most, base and depraved of all possible employments of intellectual power Nor is it by any means the most effectual way of eliciting truth. The mode best adapted for attaining this object is, I am convinced, quite different from that by which an honest, simple-minded witness is most easily baffled and confused. I have seen the experiment tried of subjecting a witness to such a kind of cross-examination by a practical lawyer as would have been, I am convinced, the most likely to alarm and perplex many an honest witness, without any effect in shaking the testimony; and afterward by a totally opposite mode of examination, such as would not at all have perplexed one who was honestly telling the truth, that same witness was drawn on, step by step, to acknowledge the utter falsity of the whole. Generally speaking, a quiet, gentle, and straightforward, though full and careful, examination will be most adapted to elicit truth, and the manoeuvres and the brow-beating which are the best adapted to confuse an honest, simple-minded witness are just what the dishonest one is the best prepared for. The more the storm blusters, the more carefully he wraps round him the cloak which a warm sunshine will induce him to throw off."

While we do not agree with all that Whately says, especially with what he says upon the treatment of a dishonest witness, his views are valuable as coming from a disinterested observer—a man of ability, who was not a lawyer. We would recommend a different course of treatment of a dishonest witness; but as we do not intend to treat fully of the subject in this place, we will only say that a bold question will sometimes lay a witness open, but the question must be sudden and unexpected, and the mind of the witness must be diverted from that part of his testimony where it is hoped to make him speak the truth, until the proper moment. An artifice mentioned by Lord Bacon is in point   He says: "When you have anything to obtain of present dispatch, you entertain and amuse the party with whom you deal with some other discourse, that he be not too much awake to make objections. I knew," he says, "a counsellor and secretary that never came to Queen Elizabeth with bills to sign, but he would always first put her into some discourse of State, that she might the less mind the bills." Such a witness may be surprised into telling the truth. The same author says: "A sudden, bold and unexpected question doth many times surprise a man and lay him open. Like to him that having changed his name, and walking in Paul's, another came suddenly behind him, and called him his true name, whereat straightways he looked back."

While witnesses are sworn to tell "the truth, the

whole truth, and nothing but the tru'n," yet there are
witnesses who believe that they are not obliged to tell
anything they are not asked about, an   if they are
undesirous of telling all they know, they will give
eva ive answers until asked about the particular thing
they wish to conceal, and then they will withhold it no
longer.   An amusing instance which illustrates what we
mean is given in one of the leading reviews, as follows:
"Some time ago the writer, while waiting in court,
watched the trial of a case where the plaintiff sought to
recover damages for a breach of warranty.   The defendant had sold him a horse with an express warranty
that he was sound and kind and free from all 'outs.'
The next day the plaintiff noticed that a shoe was loose,
and he undertook to drive him into a blacksmith's shop
to have him shod, when the horse exhibited such violent
reluctance that he was obliged to abandon the attempt.
Repeated efforts made it evident that he never would
be shod willingly, and therefore he was obliged to sell
him.   The defendant called two witnesses.   The first,
an honest, clean-looking man, testified that he was
a blacksmith, that he knew the horse in question perfectly well, and he had shod him about the time referred
to in plaintiff's testimony.   'Did you have any difficulty
in shoeing him?' asked the defendant's counsel.   'Not
the least.   He stood perfectly quiet.   Never had a horse
stand quieter.'   The other, a venerable-looking man,
with a clear blue eye, testified that he had owned the horse
and that he was perfectly kind.   'Did you ever have
any trouble about getting him into a blacksmith's shop?'
'Well, sir, I don't remember that I ever had occasion to
carry him to a blacksmith's shop while I owned him.'
The plaintiff's counsel evidently thought that cross-
examination would only develop this unpleasant testimony more strongly, so he let the witnesses go.   The
jury found for the defendant.   The next morning, as the
writer was sitting in court waiting for a verdict, a man

behind him, whom he recognised as the blacksmith, leaned forward and said · 'You heard that horse case tried yesterday, didn't you ?   Well, that fellow who tried the case for the plaintiff didn't know how to cross-examine worth a cent.   I told him that the horse stood perfectly quiet while I shod him ; and so he did.   I did not tell him I had to hold him by the nose with a pair of pincers to make him stand   The old man said he never took him to a blacksmith's shop while he had him. No more he did.   He had to take him out into an open lot and cast him before he could shoe him'" (10 *American Law Review*, 153, foot-note).

Curran's method of dealing with untruthful witnesses and those who were unwilling was often very effective. His plan is described as follows by Phillips : "At cross-examination, the most difficult, and by far the most hazardous part of a barrister's profession, he (Curran) was quite inimitable.   There was no plan which he did not detect, no web which he did not disentangle, and the unfortunate wretch, who commenced with all the confidence of preconcerted perjury, never failed to retreat before him, in all the confusion of exposure.   Indeed, it was almost impossible for the guilty to offer a successful resistance.   He argued, he cajoled, he ridiculed, he mimicked, he played off the various artillery of his talent upon the witness ; he would affect earnestness upon trifles, and levity upon subjects of the most serious import, until at length he succeeded in creating a security that was fatal, or a sullenness that produced all the consequences of prevarication.   No matter how unfair the topic, he never failed to avail himself of it ; acting upon the principle that, in law as well as war, every stratagem was admissible.   If he was hard pressed, there was no peculiarity of person, no singularity of name, no eccentricity of profession, at which he would not grasp, trying to confound the self-possession of the witness by the, no matter how excited, ridicule of the

audience." While we do not approve of the unfairness
of which Curran's biographer admits that he was guilty,
there is much to be learned by an attentive consideration
of the great advocate's method as related.

One of the most dangerous witnesses to deal with is
the witness who does not remember. The advocate
may exhaust his ingenuity, he may try every artifice of
which he is master, if the witness takes refuge behind
the convenient phrase, "I don't remember," his efforts
will be vain. He will imitate the example of Iago

> "Demand me nothing; what you know you kn
> From this time forth I never will speak word

The objects of a cross-examination are three in
number. The first is to elicit something in your favour;
the second is to weaken the force of what the witness
has said against you; and the third is to show that from
his present demeanour or from his past life he is
unworthy of belief, and thus weaken or destroy the effect
of his testimony. We shall endeavour to give in this
chapter clear and well-defined rules for the accomplishment of each of these objects. There are two modes of
cross-examining a witness pursued by accomplished
advocates. One is usually termed the savage, and the
other the smiling method, and the latter is usually to be
pursued. An adverse witness can often soften his
narrative and modify or change many things when asked
to explain them, and will do so if approached in the
proper way; but if the advocate makes an attack upon
him he will strive to injure his cause as much as possible.
Timid or diffident witnesses should not be frightened, if
they are honest. With the dishonest witness, however,
no severity of treatment can hardly be too great. But
with female, youthful, modest or aged witnesses the
advocate should deal kindly. As a matter of policy,
aside from the inhumanity and cruelty of an opposite
course, it is better to pursue this plan, and even if it

were not the best policy, an advocate can never afford to do anything unbecoming a gentleman, in the discharge of his duties, whatever they may be.

Many cases are lost by injudicious cross-examinations, and a prudent advocate will ask as few questions as possible. But while this is true, the usefulness of a cross-examination, when well conducted, must not be under-estimated. While it is true that many cases are lost by injudicious cross-examinations, perhaps a greater number are won by skilful ones. To the advocate the demeanour of the witness is of the greatest importance. If he is cunning he will endeavour to conceal his true feelings. The eye, the tones of the voice, and the mouth are the best indexes to the state of mind of a witness. A convulsive twitching of the muscles of the mouth will often betray agitation which the witness wishes to conceal, while the eye will reveal nothing as its expression may be chan   to suit the purpose of the witness. But the advocate should never take his eye from the face of a witness, for if he is seen at an unguarded moment, the expression of his eye or the movement of the muscles of the mouth will reveal the ruling sentiment of his mind. For cross-examina   n may be regarded as a mental duel between witness and advocate, and it has been said that "the advocate who takes his eyes from the witness is as likely to be worsted as the swordsman who lets his eyes wander from his adversary."

For unnumbered ages the external appearance has been deemed to be an index to the internal man, and in the Gentoo Code we find the following curious passage:

"When two persons upon a quarrel refer to arbitrators, those arbitrators at the time of examination shall observe both the plaintiff and the defendant narrowly, and take notice if either, and which of them, when he is speaking, hath his voice falter in his throat, or his colour change, or his forehead sweat, or the hair of his body stand erect, or a trembling come over his limbs, or

his eyes water, or if during the trial he cannot stand
still in his place, or frequently licks and moistens his
tongue, or hath his face grow dry, or in speaking to one
point wavers and shuffles off to another, or, if any person puts a question to him, is unable to return an
answer; from the circumstances of such commotions,
they shall distinguish the guilty party."

The signs of guilt spoken of, however, are not always
infallible, for innocent persons when unjustly accused of
crime are often so deeply mortified that they look as if
they were guilty; but notwithstanding this, the passage
quoted is worthy of the attention of the advocate.

Webster's comments upon signs of guilt exhibited, or
alleged to have been exhibited, by his clients in the
Goodrige Case, in this connection, we hope will prove
instructive :—

"The witnesses on the part of the prosecution have
testified that the defendants, when arrested, manifested
great agitation and alarm; paleness overspread their
faces, and drops of sweat stood on their temples   This
satisfied the witnesses of the defendants' guilt, and they
now state the circumstance as being indubitable proof
This argument manifests, in those who use it, equal want
of sense and sensibility.   It is precisely fitted to the
feeling and the intellect of a bum-bailiff.   In a court of
justice it deserves nothing but contempt.   Is there
nothing that can agitate the frame, or excite the blood,
but the consciousness of guilt?   If the defendants were
innocent, would they not feel indignation at this unjust
accusation?   If they saw an attempt to produce false
evidence against them, would they not be angry?   And,
seeing the production of such evidence, might they not
feel fear and alarm?   And have indignation, and anger,
and terror, no power to affect the human countenance,
or the human frame?

"Miserable, miserable, indeed, is the reasoning which
would infer any man's guilt from his agitation, when he

found himself accused of a heinous offence; when he saw evidence, which he might know to be false and fraudulent, brought against him; when his house was filled, from the garret to the cellar, by those whom he might esteem as false witnesses, and when he himself, instead of being at liberty to observe their conduct and watch their motions, was a prisoner in close custody in his own house, with the fists of a catch-poll clenched upon his throat.

"The defendants were at Newburyport the afternoon and evening of the robbery. For the greater part of the time, they show where they were and what they were doing. Their proof, it is true, does not apply to every moment. But, when it is considered that, from the moment of their arrest, they have been in close prison, perhaps they have shown as much as could be expected. Few men, when called on afterwards, can remember, and fewer still can prove, how they have passed every half-hour of an evening. At a reasonable hour they both came to the house where Laban had lodged the night before. Nothing suspicious was observed in their manners or conversation. Is it probable they would thus come unconcernedly into the company of others, from a field of robbery, and, as they must have supposed, of murder, before they could have ascertained whether the stain of blood was not on their garments? They remained in the place a part of the next day. The town was alarmed; a strict inquiry was made of all strangers, and of the defendants among others. Nothing suspicious was discovered. They avoided no inquiry, nor left the town in any haste. The jury had had an opportunity of seeing the defendants. Did their general appearance indicate that hardihood which would enable them to act this cool, unconcerned part? Was it not more likely they would have fled?"

Perjury is, as we have said, a much more uncommon crime than it is usually thought to be. Not that witnesses do not sometimes swear that which is not true, but they are often simply mistaken, and when a witness, instead of wilfully lying, is mistaken, the advocate should by a careful and patient examination prove this to the satisfaction of the jury. It is cruel, brutal, and impolitic for a lawyer to examine a witness upon the theory that he is swearing falsely when he believes that he is only mistaken as to certain immaterial matters in his testimony. Juries love fair play, and they are usually sagacious enough to discover from the demeanour of a witness whether he is swearing falsely or truly, and will govern themselves accordingly

If a witness is dishonest and not desirous of telling the truth, it is very important that he should be examined rapidly, so that he can have no time to concoct plausible answers between questions If a witness is honest he will answer the questions unhesitatingly, but if he is swearing falsely, by this method his detection will nearly always follow.

In conducting the examination of a witness who he believes has sworn falsely the advocate has two courses open to him. He may show his distrust of the witness by his manner, look, and tone of voice, or he may examine him as if he thought him an honest witness. We shall give, further on, particular directions for the guidance of the advocate in following either plan. Both courses have their advantages. The advocate, by letting the witness see that he believes he is not telling the truth, and treating him with great severity, will usually cause the witness to show his guilt by his looks, for as a general rule a liar is a moral coward. But if the witness thinks that what he has already said has been believed, he becomes careless, and if given plenty of rope he will hang himself, and the advocate can easily point out the inconsistencies in, and unreasonableness of, his testimony, to the jury in his address. When the witness has contradicted himself the advocate should not ask him to

explain, but should take advantage of the contradiction
in his argument to the jury. If asked to explain, the
witness will usually find some satisfactory explanation
even if he is obliged to invent it, take back what he has
said, or modify or change it. We think the observations
of Serjeant Ballantyne on this point, and upon the
subject of cross-examination generally, may prove instructive to our readers —

"It will not be out of place here to make some
remarks upon cross-examination. The records of Courts
of justice from all time show that truth cannot, in a
great number of cases tried, be reasonably expected.
Even when witnesses are honest and have no intention
to deceive, there is a natural tendency to exaggerate the
facts favourable to the cause for which they are appearing, and to ignore the opposite circumstances ; and the
only means known to English law by which testimony
can be sifted is cross-examination. By this agent, if
skilfully used, falsehood ought to be exposed, and
exaggerated statements reduced to their true dimensions.
An unskilful use of it, on the contrary, has a tendency
to uphold rather than destroy. If the principles upon
which cross-examination ought to be founded are not
understood and acted upon, it is worse than useless,
and it becomes an instrument against its employer.
The reckless asking of a number of questions on
the chance of getting at something is too often a
plan adopted by unskilled advocates, and noise is
mistaken for energy. Mr. Baron Alderson once
remarked to a counsel of this type, 'Mr. ——, you
seem to think that the art of cross-examination is
to examine crossly.'

"In order to attain success in this branch of advocacy,
it is necessary for counsel to form in his own mind an
opinion upon the facts of the case, and the character
and probable motives of a witness, before asking a
question. This doubtless requires experience, and the

success of his cross-examination must depend upon the accuracy of the judgment he forms.

"Great discernment is needed to distinguish material from unimportant discrepancies, and never to dwell long upon immaterial matters; but if a witness intends to commit perjury, it is rarely useful to press him upon the salient points of the case, with which he has probably made himself thoroughly acquainted, but to seek for circumstances for which he would not be likely to prepare himself. And it ought above all things to be remembered by the advocate, that when he has succeeded in making a point he should leave it alone until his turn comes to address the jury upon it. If a dishonest witness has inadvertently made an admission injurious to himself, and, by the counsel's dwelling upon it, becomes aware of the effect, he will endeavour to shuffle out of it, and perhaps succeed in doing so.

"The object of cross-examination is not to produce startling effects, but to elicit facts, which will support the theory intended to be put forward. Sir William Follett asked the fewest questions of any counsel I ever knew, and I have heard many cross-examinations from others listened to with rapture from an admiring client. Each question has been destructive to his case.

"I had put a question to a witness as to what he was doing at a particular time, this being a matter important to the inquiry. 'I was talking to a lady,' was the answer; adding, 'I will tell you who she was if you like. You know her very well' I made no observation at the time, but when addressing the jury said that my experience led me to the conclusion that honest witnesses endeavoured to keep themselves to the facts they came to prove, but that lying men endeavoured to distract the attention by introducing something irrelevant; and I think this remark is worth consideration, and points out one of the tests of truth or falsehood in the person under examination.

" Embarrassment exhibited under a searching cross-examination is not to be relied on as a proof of falsehood · the novelty of the position, or constitutional nervousness, may frequently occasion it

" I have myself succeeded, by [cross-examination, in cases where claims were made for injuries received in railway accidents, in showing that the claimant had not been present at the occurrence. Cross-examination has recently become more important than ever in sifting the evidence of professional witnesses in cases where injuries have been sustained from the above class of accidents, and in which the most eminent professional men occasionally fall into grave errors, and I feel obliged to add that some in the lower walks of the profession make the manufacture of these cases a not unprofitable trade. One of these worthies admitted in a recent trial that he might have been engaged in a hundred of them."

The advocate cross-examining a witness should conduct his examination with the testimony of the other witnesses in view, and endeavour, if possible, to secure a contradiction by the witness under examination of the other witnesses on whose side he has been called. He should also try to make the witness contradict himself, if he believes that he is lying or is mistaken No self-respecting advocate will ever try to entrap an honest witness and get him into trouble which may lead to loss of reputation, even if, by doing so, he could win the most important cause. If, however, the witness is not telling the truth, he should be exposed, or, if he is mistaken, his mistake should be explained out of his own mouth, if possible, and if a satisfactory explanation cannot be obtained, the advocate in his argument to the jury may comment with damaging effect on the mistake.

It is sometimes necessary for the advocate to show that certain facts deposed to by witnesses are impossible or at least improbable. The story of Susannah and the Elders in the Apocrypha affords an admirable example.

The two false witnesses were examined out of the hearing of each other, and on being asked under what sort of tree the criminal act was done, the first said a " mastick tree," the other a " holm tree."

"What had you for supper?" says a modern jurist. (2 Benth. Jud. Er 9) "To the merits of the cause the contents of the supper were altogether irrelevant and indifferent. But if, in speaking of a supper given on an important or recent occasion, six persons, all supposed to be present, give a different bill of fare, the contrariety affords evidence pretty satisfactory, though but of the circumstantial kind, that at least some of them were not there" The most usual application of this rule is in detection of a fabricated *alibi* This seldom succeeds if the witnesses are skilfully cross-examined out of the hearing of each other , especially as Courts and juries are aware that a false *alibi* is a favourite defence with guilty persons, and consequently listen with suspicion even to a true one.

In the examination of witnesses the advocate must not lose sight of the fact that the interest of the witness in the subject-matter of the controversy, if he is a party to the cause, or interested in the settlement of a question which arises in the case, or if he is related by consanguinity or affinity to the party in whose favour he has been called, or is at enmity with the party against whom he is testifying, or the friend or enemy of either of the parties, will be apt to colour his story, and make it favourable or unfavourable according to the interest or bias of the witness. And this is often true when the witness is honest. By exaggeration, evasion, equivocation, indistinctness or pretended want of memory, a witness may do great damage to the side which he is called to assist. If the advocate is as familiar with all the facts of the case as he should be, he can usually take advantage of these things by showing that his testimony does not agree with the facts as deposed to by the other witnesses.

One of the most effective ways to discredit a witness is to inquire closely into the sources of his knowledge For instance, when a witness has given, in detail, a narrative of a past transaction and you wish to show to the Court and jury that he was mistaken, you should picture the scene in your own mind, place, persons and accessories You should then have the witness repeat his narrative, taking care to note its congruity or want of congruity with the accompanying circumstances, then you are apt to detect improbabilities and even impossibilities. You put yourself in the place of the witness, and see as he saw, you notice how he was prejudiced, how he formed too hasty conclusions, etc. We all know how erring the senses are and how unreliable and frail the human memory is.

It is said that Sir Walter Raleigh tore up the manuscript of the second volume of his " History of the World," because he was unable to ascertain the true cause of a fight which took place under his own observation beneath the window of his room in the tower where he was imprisoned, remarking that if he could not obtain an accurate account of such an occurrence, it must be impossible to give a correct narrative of events which occurred in ages long past and in remote quarters of the globe.

Where honest witnesses make conflicting statements, and it is necessary to ascertain which of them has sworn truly, much depends upon the powers of perception and memory of the witnesses, and upon their ability to narrate correctly the events which they witnessed, for in order to give a true account of what he has seen, a witness must have a correct perception of what he saw, and a memory which is *retentive enough* to enable him to *recall* with *accuracy* all that passed in his presence. The line of demarcation between imagination and memory, however, is sometimes hard to draw, and it is unquestionably true that witnesses testify

to things which they imagine have occurred, but which
in fact have had no existence : the memory is deceitful
and unreliable, and the things which are stored away in
it receive colour from existing impressions and experi-
ences; the new things are mingled with the old. A
writer of ability says upon this matter. "Men have
seen a very simple fact, gradually when it is distant, in
thinking of it, they interpret it, amplify it, provide it
with details, and these imaginary details become incor-
porated with the details, and seem themselves to be
recollections." An instance is related by Ram of witnesses in a trial in Scotland, who were unable to separate
what they had read in a newspaper from what they
had heard from the parties. The experienced cross-
examiner, therefore, will not take the statements of
honest witnesses for granted, but will investigate them
thoroughly, and endeavour to show that they are
mistaken as to what they think they heard or saw, and
will, in the mildest and most patient manner, prove, by
his examination of a witness who believes that he is
telling the truth, that, from the surrounding circumstances
and the testimony of the other witnesses as well as from
the unreasonableness of his story, his evidence cannot
be relied upon.

The language used by counsel in England a few
centuries ago, would not now be tolerated in a Court of
justice. We can hardly conceive how a man of Lord
Coke's ability could display such violent temper in the
conduct of a cause, and it is difficult to assign any
adequate cause for the indecent eagerness with which he
pressed the case against Sir Walter Raleigh, and for the
harsh and cruel language with which he assailed him.
In the course of Coke's address Raleigh interrupted him.
"To whom speak you this? You tell me news I never
heard of." To which Coke replied. "Oh, sir, do I?
I will prove you the notoriest traitor that ever came to
the bar. After you have taken away the King, you

would alter religion, as you, Sir Walter Raleigh, have followed them of the bye in imitation, for I will charge you with the words." "Your words cannot condemn me," said Raleigh; "my innocence is my defence. Prove one of those things wherewith you have charged me, and I will confess the whole indictment, and that I am the horriblest traitor that ever lived, and worthy to be crucified with a thousand cruel torments"—"Nay," answered Coke, "I will prove all.—Thou art a monster; thou hast an English face but a Spanish heart.—Now you must have money. Armberg was no sooner in England (I charge thee, Raleigh) but thou incitest Cobham to go unto him, and to deal with him for money, to bestow on discontented persons to raise rebellion in the kingdom."—"Let me answer for myself," said Raleigh.—"Thou shalt not," was the fierce and brutal reply of Coke. Again, on Raleigh observing that the guilt of Lord Cobham was no evidence against himself, Coke replied: "All that he did was by thy instigation, thou viper! for I *thou* thee, thou traitor."—"It becometh not a man of virtue and quality to call me so," was Raleigh's dignified rebuke, "but I take comfort in it, it is all you can do"—"Have I angered you?" said Coke.—"I am in no case to be angry," was Raleigh's answer. In other instances, during the trial, similar language was held by Coke towards the prisoner, till at length Cecil observed. "Be not so impatient, Mr. Attorney-General; give him leave to speak." On this rebuke Coke sat down in anger, and was with difficulty persuaded to proceed. When, at length, he resumed, he burst forth into a fresh torrent of invective, accusing Raleigh, not only of the darkest treasons, but applying to him the epithet of "damnable atheist." Nor was it merely by the intemperance of his language that Coke on this occasion disgraced himself. He adduced evidence against the prisoner, which, even in the then lax practice in the case of trials for treason, was obviously illegal.

The declarations of living witnesses were brought forward, and it was principally upon this proof that the prisoner was convicted. Many years after this conviction, and notwithstanding the implied pardon upon which Raleigh insisted, arising out of his subsequent employment under the Crown, he was brought before the Court of King's Bench to have execution awarded against him ; and upon this occasion Sir Edward Coke, who presided as Chief Justice, retracted the slander which he had cast on the religious opinions of the prisoner. " I know," said he, addressing Raleigh, " you have been valiant and wise, and I doubt not you retain both these virtues, for now you shall have occasion to use them. Your faith hath heretofore been questioned, but I am resolved you are a good Christian, for your book, which is an admirable work, doth testify as much." (State Trials, vol. 11, p. 35, footnote)

Many cases are lost by injudicious attacks upon the credit of witnesses upon cross-examination. Parties to causes are often actuated by feelings of the bitterest enmity to each other, and they allow their passions to cloud their judgments, and become not only intent upon winning their cases, but upon destroying the characters of their opponents. No advocate should allow himself to become an instrument of vengeance in the hands of his irate clients. If he will allow them to do so, they will often dictate to him the questions to be asked upon cross-examination, and will become seriously offended if he does not ask them, but the advocate is unworthy of his profession if he becomes basely subservient to his client under such circumstances. He should plainly tell his client that he cannot submit to such dictation, and that he shall pursue the course which seems to him to be proper.

Juries are quick to resent unwarranted attacks upon the character of witnesses or parties upon cross-examination, and in estimating the damages to a plaintiff they will usually give him damages not only for the original wrong which he has suffered at the hands of the defendant, but they will also give him damages which have been done his character by a virulent cross-examination, or a malignant attack upon him made by counsel in his address to the jury

In this connection Sir Frank Lockwood, in the course of the address to which reference has been made on page 36, said ·—

"Then they approached the cross-examination. He admitted it to be a difficult question, and it was rendered all the more difficult perhaps by the crusade which had been warred lately in the public press against cross-examination. According to the public press there were a lot of swashbucklers going about the world disguised as lawyers, who endeavoured to get their living by the injury of reputations, by cruel attacks upon credit. Those whom he was addressing knew perfectly well that any man who so betrayed a professional trust that was placed within his hands was not only a knave, but a fool. Whoever had been in the habit of going into a Court of justice knew perfectly well that cruel and irrelevant cross-examination was disastrous to the cause whose advocate administered it. He believed that if cross-examination was improper, or irrelevant, or cruel, it brought its punishment at once, and he was certain that the cause was lost that was endeavoured to be bolstered up by it. No one knew better than the distinguished advocates he saw around him when to stop in a cross-examination. The hint came from the jury-box before much mischief was done, and the advocate was a bad one who did not take the hint. He would give them another piece of advice as to when to cease cross-examination Never continue the cross-examination of a witness if they saw the Judge showed the slightest disposition to do it himself If they saw the Judge, to use a somewhat sporting expression, in the least inclined to take up the running, let him do it. He would do it

much better, much more effectively than they could do
it, because he would undertake to say that there was not
one of Her Majesty's Judges sitting on the Bench who,
if he chose, could not mar the best cross-examination
that could be administered   A witness could not be
cross-examined without the approval of the Bench ; with
the approval of the Bench one could do pretty much
what one liked.   Then, again, in cross-examination
there must be some sense of proportion.   When they
were attacking credit, it was a blunder to rake up old
stories if they could help it.   Nothing was more dis-
tasteful to a jury.   If on reflection they believed it was
their duty to do it, let them do it fearlessly, and no
honest man would blame them."

Of course, there are times when the credit of a witness
should be impeached by showing that, from his history,
he is not a man likely to swear the truth if it becomes
to his interest to swear to the contrary , but unless the
offence which he has committed, or is supposed to have
committed, be of recent occurrence, and of a heinous
nature, it would be wiser to ask no questions concerning it.

It is often cruel and inhuman for counsel to unearth
errors of conduct which have been committed many
years before, and which, perhaps, have been sincerely
repented of, by the offender.   It seems to us inexcusable
for an advocate to pursue this course, and cause a human
being who is trying to live honestly and to demean
himself as a good citizen, and who has turned from his
evil ways, to despair of ever regaining the goodwill and
esteem of his fellow-men, and to bring him into contempt
and ridicule in the community in which he lives, and
even cause him to be despised by the wife of his bosom
and hated by his offspring.   Of what use is it to repent
of evil conduct, if there are none to complete the refor-
mation of the offender by lending him a helping hand ?
This unwillingness upon the part of society to forgive

youthful offences, or errors committed in a moment of passion, has caused many men who would have been ornaments of society if kindly treated, to become festering sores upon the body politic and criminals of the most hardened type and dangerous enemies of their kind. It would be better to impose capital punishment for the most trivial offences, and re-enact the bloody Draconian code, than to punish offenders by such diabolical means and cause them to suffer pangs a thousand times more excruciatingly painful than those of death itself.

But if the advocate is not restrained by such considerations as these, let him reflect that throwing mud is a game that two can play at, and that for a man who lives in a glass house to throw stones is a foolish thing, for, where one side assails the credit of a witness or party to a cause, the other side through feelings of revenge, is apt to do the same thing, and when this is the case what a pitiable spectacle is often presented! Then the skeletons which are supposed to lurk in all family closets are brought forth to the light of day. As sensible would be the conduct of patients in a hospital who, moved by anger, should spring from their beds of pain, and tear the bandages from each other's wounds and expose them to the gaze of the gaping multitude in all their ghastly hideousness.

The ability to cross-examine professional expert witnesses well, is rare. It has been the habit, of late, to speak slightingly of the testimony of this class of witnesses, some of the Courts both in England and in the United States have very plainly intimated that they consider the testimony of this class of witnesses very unreliable. And in one of the leading American law magazines a professional expert witness has been defined to be "a man who is paid a retainer to make a sworn argument." (27 Am. Law Reg, iii, footnote.) While expert witnesses are often biassed in favour of the side by which they are

called, and show great zeal in endeavouring to sub-
stantiate the propositions contended for by it, we are
inclined to believe that, as a general rule, too little
weight is given to the testimony of experts. The time
has been when, perhaps, it was given too great a weight
by the Courts, but we are constrained to believe that
some of the utterances of Judges have not been weighed
with due care when speaking upon this subject.

The only safe way for an advocate who has an expert
to deal with upon cross-examination, is to hold him
down to the issues involved and not allow him to
cover too much ground, nor to argue the case of
the party who has called his services into requisition.
Experts are, as a class, shrewd and cunning, and are
usually selected on account of their eminence in their
professions, or skill in their avocations, and they are
presumed to speak guardedly and carefully upon topics
with which they have the greatest familiarity, for they
often stake their reputations upon the result of the trial
in which they are called to testify. Hence the advocate,
whose duty it becomes to examine witnesses of the kind,
cannot come to the performance of his task with too much
information upon the subject under investigation.

The best method of examining witnesses of this
character is to take advantage of their enthusiasm in the
cause of the party whose side they are to maintain, and
quietly and gradually lead them to an extreme position
which can neither be fortified nor successfully defended.
They usually take pleasure in imparting their knowledge
to others while upon the stand, for they have a large
share of that vanity which Max O'Rell attributes to
every American citizen, when he says, "that in America
every fellow wishes every other fellow to think that he
is a devil of a fellow," and this fondness for display and
love of approbation will often cause them to get into very
deep water ; but in order that the advocate may accomplish his purpose he must conceal the object he has in

view, and remain master of himself no matter how trying his situation may prove. He must, then, when he has led the witness to make statements which are improbable and unreasonable, ask him to explain his glaring inaccuracies, and if he attempts to equivocate or give evasive answers, sternly hold him to the issues involved. In this way many experts are completely broken down and their testimony is rendered worthless to the side for which they are called.

But it often happens that so-called experts are mere shams and pretenders, and utterly unqualified to express an opinion upon the subject under investigation. When this is the case it is often wise not to object to the witness testifying as an expert upon the ground of incompetency, if he should happen to be technically qualified, for jurors often being self-made men, are sometimes sensitive upon this point. Many of them think that a practical knowledge of things can be acquired by experience better than by a thorough course of instruction in the best institution of learning; consequently, with this in mind, the advocate would do well to allow the witness to stand upon his merits, and by a searching examination prove that he does not know so much as he thinks he does about the questions involved.

But if the testimony of an expert witness is not to be shaken, it is better to examine him upon a few unimportant matters, to show the jury you are not afraid to question him, and then dismiss him.

In questioning witnesses upon cross-examination, advocates will find it a good plan to ask the most important questions as if they were the most unimportant, and in fact, to appear to the witness to want exactly the opposite of what they really want to get out of him

This course is often pursued by some of the most successful advocates.

Judge Elliot, the able and learned writer upon the

subject of advocacy, speaking of the duty of opposing counsel while his witness is being cross-examined, to watch narrowly the questions which are put to his witness, says : "It is a common practice for some not over-scrupulous advocates to ask unfair questions. Even so great, and usually so fair an advocate as Erskine was admonished to give the witness fair play. Fair play every witness is entitled to, and fair play the counsel who calls him should see that he gets. It is no unusual thing to assume that the witness has made a statement that he did not make, and on this false assumption harass and confuse him. A witness, be it always remembered, is not generally self-possessed under the fire of a hot cross-examination, and may be bewildered by such an assumption, made, as most often it is, with a dogmatic and determined air. Such assumptions counsel have no right to make."

More unfair and more perplexing to the witness, as well as more difficult for the advocate to detect, are those insidious questions in which the assumption is covertly made. It is no uncommon thing for cross-examiners to bewilder witnesses by questions which covertly assume a fact that dare not be openly assumed. Many a disputant with far better opportunities for deliberation and reflection has been hopelessly entangled by these unfair questions The authors of the "Port Royal Logic" give this example · " In the same way, if, knowing the probity of a Judge, any one should ask me if he sold justice still, I could not reply by simply saying ' no,' since the ' no ' would signify that he did not sell it now, but would leave it to be inferred, at the same time, that I allowed that he had formerly sold it " To this class belong such questions as · "When did you cease to be the enemy of the plaintiff ? " "When did you sell your interest in this claim ? " "When did you retire from the conspiracy ? " "When did you convert the horse ? "

This unfair method of examination sometimes takes

the form of a question which, in appearance, is one question only, demanding simply a categorical answer, whereas, in reality, several questions are combined. This is an old fallacy, and ought to be so well known as to be readily exposed, but it does, nevertheless, yet do no little mischief. Many a witness has been sorely puzzled by being required to answer "yes" or "no" to a question which in form is single, but in fact is double Thus, a witness is asked : "You hurt yourself by jumping off a train running forty miles an hour ?" Or he is asked "You paid the money to the plaintiff's agent ?" Or again he is asked · "You were the plaintiff's partner in the venture ' " If the one to whom are addressed questions so plainly double as these were cool and collected, doubtless he would not be misled ; but few witnesses can be cool and collected under cross-examination, and they are often betrayed into error. A witness who has an advocate demanding of him, "Answer yes or no, sir," is not in a condition to clearly perceive the unfairness of the question asked him. Nor are the questions ordinarily asked of witnesses so plainly double as these we have given by way of illustration, for many are so adroitly constructed as to deceive keen thinkers. The remedy for this evil is that proposed by Aristotle : "Several questions," he says, "should be at once decomposed into their several parts. Only a single question admits of a single answer." We commend this advice to our readers. They will find it useful in practice.

It may not be out of place to suggest here, that much greater latitude is given on cross-examination than on examination in chief, but that a witness may not be cross-examined as to collateral and irrelevant matters merely for the purpose of afterward contradicting or impeaching him, *ante*, pp. 23, 24, 64.

The fact that jurors are governed, to a great extent, in giving or refusing credence to the statements of witnesses by their reputation, their demeanour in the box, etc., should not be lost sight of by the cross-examiner. He should be careful not to treat an honest witness as if he were dishonest, for if he does, he will do his case incalculable harm.

Much depends upon his judgment, for no general rule will be found at all times a safe guide.

The improbability or impossibility of the statements of witnesses will often furnish an advocate with a clue which, if followed, will lead to valuable results. In his treatise on "Legal Ethics" Judge Sharswoods gives an instance of a reckless swearer being brought to grief by a skilful cross-examination, which we will give in his own words :

" He [a gentleman of the Bar of Philadelphia] allowed nothing that occurred in a cause to disturb or surprise him On an occasion in one of the neighbouring counties, the circuit of which it was his custom to ride, he was trying a cause on a bond when a witness for defendant was introduced, who testified that the defendant had taken the amount of the bond, which was quite a large sum, from his residence to that of the obligee, a distance of several miles, and paid him in silver in his presence The evidence was totally unexpected ; his clients were orphan children, all their fortune was staked on this case The witness had not yet committed himself as to how the money was carried. Without any discomposure, without lifting his eyes, or pen from paper, he made on the margin of his notes of trial a calculation of what the amount in silver would weigh, and when it came his turn to cross-examine calmly proceeded to make the witness repeat his testimony step by step—when, where, how, and how far the money was carried, and then asked him if he knew how much that sum of money weighed , and upon naming the amount, so confounded the witness, party, and counsel engaged for the defendant, that the defence was at once abandoned, and a verdict for the plaintiff rendered on the spot."

"Rufus Choate is a wonderful man ; he is a marvel," said Daniel Webster to a friend in Washington some time before his death. Webster's opinion of Choate, who was one of his dearest friends, was the unanimous opinion of those of his professional brethren who knew him intimately. His method of cross-examination will prove instructive and interesting to our readers. One of his biographers says of him. "But his cross-examination was a model. As was said, in speaking of his conversations, he never assaulted a witness as if determined to browbeat him. He commented to me once on the cross-examinations of a certain eminent counsellor at our Bar with decided disapprobation. Said he 'This man goes at a witness in such a way that he inevitably gets the jury all on the side of the witness. I do not,' he added, 'think that is a good plan.' His own plan was far more wary, intelligent and circumspect. He had a profound knowledge of human nature, of the springs of human action, of the thoughts of human hearts. To get at these and make them patent to the jury, he would ask only a few telling questions—a very few questions—but generally every one of them was fired point-blank and hit the mark. He has told me, 'Never cross-examine any more than is absolutely necessary. If you don't break your witness he breaks you; *for he only repeats over in stronger language to the jury his story.* Thus you only give him a second chance to tell his story to them, and besides, by some random question you may draw out something damaging to your own case.' This last is a frightful liability. Except in occasional cases, his cross-examinations were as short as his arguments were long. He treated every man who appeared like a fair and honest person on the stand, as if upon the presumption that he was a gentleman ; and if a man appeared badly, he demolished him ; but with the air of a surgeon performing a disagreeable amputation—as if he was profoundly sorry for the necessity

Few men, good or bad, ever cherished any resent-
ment against Choate for his cross examination of them.
His whole style of address to the occupants of the
witness stand was soothing, kind and reassuring. When
he came down heavily to crush a witness, it was with a
calm, resolute decision, but no asperity—nothing curt,
nothing tart.

"I never saw any witness get the better of him in an
encounter of art or impudence. Very rarely, if ever, did
he get the laugh of the court-room fairly against him. He
had all the adroitness of the Greek Pericles, of whom
his adversary said, that he could throw Pericles, but
when he did throw him he insisted upon it that he never
was down, and he persuaded the *very spectators to
believe him.* Occasionally Mr. Choate would catch a
Tartar, as the phrase goes, in his cross-examinations.
In a District Court case, he was examining a government witness, a seaman who had turned States evidence
against his comrades who had stolen monies from the
ship on a distant shore The witness stated that the
other defendant, Mr Choate's client, instigated the
deed. 'Well,' asked Choate, 'what did he say? Tell
us *how* and *what* he spoke to you.' 'Why,' said the
witness, 'he told us there was a man in Boston named
Choate, and he'd get us off if they caught us *with the
money in our boots*' Of course a prodigious roar of
mirth followed this truthful satire , but Choate sat still
bolt upright, and perfectly imperturbable. His sallow
face twisted its corrugations a little more deeply; but
he uttered the next question calmly, coolly, and with
absolute intrepidity of assurance."

Men of the greatest ability and experience often
dread the ordeal of cross-examination. Constitutionally
nervous and timid, they shrink from the cross-examinations of those advocates who have the reputation of
being severe. A singular instance of this is given by
Phillips in his work on "Curran and his Contemporaries,"

in relation to the dread of Chief Justice Bushe to pass the ordeal of cross examination by Lord Brougham. The author says: "Never shall I forget the state of nervous excitement into which he worked himself, on being summoned to give evidence before the Irish Committee in the House of Lords, in 1839. I think I see him at this moment, as I saw him then, hawking his carpet bag full of documents up and down the corridors, now walking himself out of breath, now pausing to recover it, now eyeing the bag on which he much counted, and again gazing about in absolute bewilderment. At last in much perturbation he exclaimed: 'The character of a witness is new to me, Phillips. I am familiar with nothing here. The matter on which I come is most important I need all my self-possession, and yet I protest to you I have only one idea, and that is, *Lord Brougham cross-examining me*'"

During the trial of the case of *Tilton* v. *Beecher*, in the cross-examination of Mr. Beecher by Mr. Fullerton, of counsel for the plaintiff, who has an excellent reputation as a cross-examiner, the counsel found fault with the hesitancy of the eloquent and able divine in not answering his questions more freely and directly, and the reply was made: "*I am afraid of you.*" Perhaps the novelty of the situation is the cause of the embarrassment of witnesses who under other circumstances are entirely free from it. This effect of a person in an unaccustomed situation is noticed by Anthony Trollope in one of his novels —

"I always like to get him (Hopkins the gardener) into the house, because he feels himself a little abashed by the chairs and tables , or, perhaps it is the carpet that is too much for him. Out on the gravel walks he is such a terrible tyrant, and in the greenhouse he almost tramples on one."

It will be readily seen, then, that the position of a witness under the fire of a severe cross-examination is unenviable. Mr. Beecher, on the platform as a lecturer, in the pulpit as a preacher of the highest oratorical talent, and in the social circle, was one of the most self-possessed men that could have been found.   If distinguished men, like Bushe and Beecher, were frightened at the idea of submitting to cross-examination, what must be the feelings of delicate women and young persons who are sworn for the first time, and who are unaccustomed to the publicity incident to the trial of a cause in one of our Courts?   How inexcusable, then, must be the conduct of advocates who handle such witnesses roughly in their cross-examinations !

But, while it is true that the right of cross-examination is sometimes abused, the value of its legitimate use as a means of investigating truth, under our system of government, cannot be over-estimated.   The origin of the right of cross-examination is lost in the dim mists of antiquity, but that it is of ancient origin there can be no doubt.   Solomon seems to have favoured it as a means of establishing truth, for he says. "He that is first in his own cause seemeth just, *but his neighbour cometh and searcheth him.*"

We know of no more valuable rules for the cross-examination of a witness than those laid down by David Paul Brown, and those given by Mr Cox, in his admirable work entitled, "The Advocate his Training, Practice, Rights and Duties," and as this book is not to be found easily, we have deemed it advisable to give his rules in full.

We will first give the deservedly famous Golden Rules for the cross-examination of a witness by David Paul Brown —

I —Except in indifferent matters, never take your eye from that of the witness; this is a channel of communication from mind to mind, the loss of which nothing can compensate.

  " Truth, falsehood, hatred, anger, scorn, despair,
   And all the passions—all the soul is there

II.—Be not regardless of the *voice* of the witness ; next to the eye, this is perhaps the best interpreter of his mind. The very design to screen conscience from crime —the mental reservation of the witness—is often manifested in the tone or accent or emphasis of the voice. For instance, it becoming important to know that the witness was at the corner of Sixth and Chestnut Streets at a certain time, the question is asked, Were you at the corner of Sixth and Chestnut Streets at six o'clock ? A frank witness would answer—perhaps—I was near there. But a witness who had been there, desirous to conceal the fact, and to defeat your object, speaking to the letter rather than the spirit of the inquiry, answers No , although he may have been within a stone's throw of the place, or at the very place, within ten minutes of the time. The common answer of such a witness would be : " I was not at the *corner* at *six o'clock*."

Emphasis upon both words plainly implies a mental evasion or equivocation, and gives rise with a skilful examiner to the question · "At what hour were you at the corner?" or, "At what place were you at six o'clock ?" And in nine instances out of ten it will appear, that the witness was at the place at the time, or at the time about the place   There is no scope for further illustration— but be watchful, I say, of the voice, and the principle may be easily applied.

III —Be mild with the mild—shrewd with the crafty —confiding with the honest—merciful to the young, the frail, or the fearful—rough to the ruffian and a thunderbolt to the liar. But in all this, never be unmindful of your own dignity. Bring to bear all the powers of your mind—not that *you* may shine, but that *virtue* may triumph, and your *cause* may prosper.

IV.—In a *criminal*, especially in a *capital* case, so long as your cause stands well, ask but few questions; and be certain never to ask any, the answer to which, if against you, may destroy your client, unless you know the witness *perfectly* well, and know that his answer will be favourable *equally* well, or unless you be prepared with testimony to destroy him, if he play traitor to the truth and your expectations.

V.—An equivocal question is almost as much to be avoided and condemned as an equivocal answer. Singleness of purpose, clearly expressed, is the best trial in the examination of witnesses, whether they be honest or the reverse. Falsehood is not detected by cunning, but by the light of truth, or if by cunning, it is the cunning of the witness, and not of the counsel

VI.—If the witness determine to be witty or refractory with you, you had better settle that account with him at *first*, or its items will increase with the examination Let him have an opportunity of satisfying himself either that he has mistaken *your* power, or his *own*. But in any result be careful that you do not lose your temper , anger is always either the precursor or evidence of assured defeat in every intellectual conflict.

VII.—Like a skilful chess-player, in every move fix your mind upon the combinations and relations of the game—partial and temporary success may otherwise end in total and remediless defeat.

VIII.—Never undervalue your adversary, but stand steadily upon your guard , a random blow may be just as fatal as though it were directed by the most consummate skill; the negligence of one often cures and sometimes renders effective the blunders of another

IX.—Be respectful to the Court and to the jury, kind to your colleague, civil to your antagonist , but never sacrifice the slightest principle of duty to an overweening deference toward either.

The rules given by Mr. Cox for the cross-examination of witnesses are as follows —

" Cross-examination is commonly esteemed the severest test of an advocate's skill, and perhaps it demands beyond any other of his duties the exercise of his *ingenuity* But the experienced will doubt whether, upon the whole, it is so difficult to do well as an examination in chief, and certainly it is more frequently well done, although this may not improbably result from the prevalent notion that examination in chief is an easy matter, which anybody can do, while cross-examination is extremely difficult ; and therefore the advocates, and especially young advocates, perform the one carelessly, while they put forth all their powers for the accomplishment of the other.

"Do not understand, however, that we are unconscious of the difficulty of conducting a cross-examination with creditable skill. It is undoubtedly a great intellectual effort ; it is the direct conflict of mind with mind, it demands, not merely much knowledge of the human mind, its faculties, and their *modus operandi*, to be learned only by reading, reflection and observation, but much experience of man and his motives derived from intercourse with various classes and many persons, and, above all, by that practical experience in the art of dealing with witnesses, which is worth more than all other knowledge, which other knowledge will materially assist, but without which no amount of study will suffice to accomplish an advocate.

"To the onlooker, a cross-examination has much more of interest, for it is more in the nature of a combat, with the excitement that always attends a combat of any kind, physical or intellectual—man against man, mind wrestling with mind. Whereas, in examination in chief, the advocate and his witness have the appearance, at least, of being allies, and whatever skill the former is required to exercise for the attainment of his object needs to be concealed, and is seldom apparent to a mere spectator, however it may be recognised and appreciated by those who are engaged with him in the cause, and who know with what exquisite tact he has elicited just what he desired, and suppressed that which he wanted not to reveal.

"There are two *styles* of cross-examination, which we may term the savage style and the smiling style. The aim of the savage style is to terrify the witness into telling the truth; the aim of the smiling style is to win him to a confession. The former is by far the most frequently in use, especially by young advocates, who probably imagine that a frown and a fierce voice are proofs of power. Great is their mistake The passions rouse the passions. Anger, real or assumed, kindles anger. An attack stimulates to defiance. By showing suspicion of a witness, you insult his self-love—you make him your enemy at once—you arm his resolution to resist you—to defy you—to tell you no more than he is obliged to tell—to defeat you if he can

"Undoubtedly there are cases where such a tone is called for, where it is politic as well as just; but they are rare, so rare that they should be deemed entirely exceptional. In every part of an advocate's career, good temper and self-command are essential qualifications, but in none more so than in the practice of cross-examination.

"It is marvellous how much may be accomplished with the most difficult witness, simply by good humour and a smile, a tone of friendliness will often succeed in obtaining a reply which has been obstinately denied to a surly aspect, and a threatening or reproachful voice. As a general rule, subject to such very rare exceptions as scarcely to enter into your calculations, you should begin your cross-examination with an encouraging look, and manner, and phrase. Remember that the witness knows you to be on the other side; he is prepared to deal with you as an enemy; he anticipates a badgering; he thinks you are going to trip him up, if you can; he has, more or less, girded himself for the strife. It is amusing to mark the instant change in the demeanour of most witnesses when their own counsel has resumed his seat, and the advocate on the other side rises to cross-examine. The position, the countenance, plainly show what is passing in the mind. Either there is fear, or, more often, defiance. If you look fierce and look sternly, it is just what had been expected, and you are met by corresponding acts of self-defence. But if, instead of this, you wear a pleasant smile, speak in a kindly tone, use the language of a friendly questioner, appear to give him credit for a desire to tell the whole truth, you surprise, you disarm him ; it is not what he had anticipated, and he answers frankly your questionings.

"But where shall you begin ? What order shall you follow ? Shall you carry him again through the narrative given in his examination in chief, or begin at the end of it and go backwards, or dodge him about, now here, now there, without method ?

"Each of these plans has its advantages, and perhaps each should be adopted according to the special circumstances of the particular case.

"But you cannot determine which course to adopt, unless you have some definite design in the questions you are about to put. A mere aimless, haphazard cross-examination is a fault every advocate should strenuously guard against. It is far better to say nothing than to risk the consequence of random shots, which may as often wound your friends as your opponents. Very little experience in civil or criminal Courts, and in the latter especially, will assure you that there is no error so common as this. Some persons seem to suppose that their credit is concerned in getting up a cross-examination, and they look upon the dismissal of a witness without it as if it were an opportunity lost, and they feared that clients would attribute it, not so much to prudence as to conscious incapacity. So they rise and put a number of questions that do not concern the issue, and perhaps elicit something more damaging to their own cause than anything the other side has brought out, and the result is, that they have their client in a far worse condition than before. Let it be a rule with you *never to cross-examine unless you have some distinct object to gain by it.* Far better be mute through the whole trial, dismissing every witness without a word, than, for the mere sake of appearances, to ply them with questions not the result of a purpose You will not fall in the estimation of those on whom your fortunes will depend ; but the contrary. The attorneys well know that in legal conflicts, even more than in military ones, discretion is the better part of valour; they will not mistake the motive of your silence, but they will commend the prudence whose wisdom is proved by the results. Your first resolve will therefore be, *whether you will cross-examine at all.* It is impossible to prescribe any rule to guide you in this; so much must depend upon the particular circumstances of each case. You must rely upon your own sagacity, on a hasty review of what the witness has said—how his testimony has affected your case, and what probability there is of your weakening what he has said If he has said nothing material, usually the safer course is to let him go without a question, unless indeed you are instructed that he can give some testimony in your favour, or damaging to the party who has called him, and then you should proceed to draw that out of him. But unless so instructed, you should not, on some mere vague suspicions of your own, or in hope of hitting a blot somewhere by accident, incur the hazard of eliciting something damaging to you—a result to be seen every day in our Courts. So, as a general rule, it is dangerous to cross-examine witnesses called for mere formal proofs, as to prove signatures, attestations, copies, and such like Still, such witnesses are not to be immediately dismissed, for you should first consider if there be any similar parts of your case which they may prove, so as to save a witness to you and then you should carefully confine yourself to the purpose for which you have detained them.

"In resolving whether or not to cross-examine a witness, it is necessary to remember that there can be but three objects in cross-examination It is designed either to destroy or weaken the force of the evidence the witness has already given against you, or to elicit something in your favour which he has not stated, or to discredit him by showing to the jury, from his past history or present demeanour, that he is unworthy of belief. Never should you enter upon a cross-examination without having a clear purpose to pursue one or all of these objects. If you have not such, keep your seat

" Let us consider each of these objects of cross-examination separately —

" 1. *To destroy or weaken the force of his testimony in favour of the other side.* If this be your design, you can attain it only by one of two processes. You must show from the witness's own lips, either that what he has stated is false, or that it is capable of explanation.

" If your opinion be that he is honest but prejudiced; that he is mistaken ; that he has formed a too hasty judgment, and so forth, your bearing towards him cannot be too gentle, kind and conciliatory. Approach him with a smile, encourage him with a cheering word, assure him that you are satisfied that he intends to tell the truth and the whole truth, and having thus won his good-will and confidence, proceed slowly, quietly, and in a tone as conversational as possible to your object. Do not approach it too suddenly, or you will chance to frighten him with that which forms the greatest impediment to the discovery of the truth from a witness, the dread of appearing to contradict himself If once this alarm be kindled, it is extremely difficult to procure plain, unequivocal answers The witness forthwith places himself on the defensive, and, deeming you an enemy, fences you with more or less of skill, certainly, but always to the weakening of whatever may drop from him in your favour With such a witness, of whose candour you are seeking to avail yourself, the better course is to begin with the beginning of the story he has told, and conduct him through it again in the same order, only introducing at the right places the questions which are intended to explain or qualify what he has stated in his examination in chief The advantage of this course is the avoidance of any appearance of a surprise upon him. You take him into his former track—you even make him repeat a portion of what he has before said—you recall his mind to the subject with which it is familiar. The scene is again before him, occupying his thoughts. Then it is easy to try him upon the details (but still gently), to suggest whether it may not have differed by so-and-so from that which he has described, or if so-and-so (which gives the transaction another complexion) did not occur also, and thus at more or less length according to the circumstances of the case.

"And here, at the very outset, let us warn you against exhibiting any kind of emotion during cross-examination; especially to avoid the slightest show of exultation when the witness answers to your sagacious touch, and reveals what apparently he intended to conceal. It startles him into self-command, and closes the portal of his mind against you more closely than ever.

"You have put him upon his guard and defeated yourself. Let the most important answer appear to be received as calmly and unconsciously as if it were the most trivial of gossip

"In the same manner you may carry him to the conclusion of his story, and what with an explanation of one fact, and addition to another, and a toning down of the colour of the whole, the evidence will usually appear in a very different aspect after a judicious cross-examination, from that which it wore at the close of the examination in chief

"Thus you should deal with a witness whom you believe to be truthful, and therefore from whom you propose only to elicit explanations and facts in your favour which the opposite counsel has not, of course, assisted him to disclose.

"If you suspect that some of the statements of the witness are false in fact although not wilfully misstated—errors of the senses, of the imagination, of the memory—so much more frequent than they whose occupation has not been to sift and weigh the worth of evidence might suppose—your task becomes a very difficult one, for without in any manner charging him with perjury, or desiring to have it understood that you do otherwise than believe him to be an honest witness, you have to prevail upon him to confess that which will wear the aspect of falsehood. Now there is nothing upon which witnesses of every grade of rank and intellect are so sensitive as self-contradiction. They suspect your purpose instantly, and the dread of being made to appear as lying, while often producing contradiction and evasion, more often arms the resolution of the witness to adhere to his original statement, without qualification or explanation. When, therefore, it is your purpose to show from the witness's own lips that he was mistaken, the extremest caution is required in approaching him. You must wear an open brow, and assume a kindly tone. Let there be in your language no sound of suspicion. Intimate to him delicately your confidence that he is desirous of telling the truth, and the whole truth. Be careful not to frighten him by point-blank questions going at once to involve him in a contradiction or he will see your design, and thwart it by a resolute adhesion to his first assertion. You must approach the object under cover, opening with some questions that relate to other matter, and then gradually coming round to the desired point, and even when you have neared the desired point you must endeavour, by every device your ingenuity can suggest, to avoid the direct question, the answer to which necessarily and obviously involves the contradiction. The safer and surer course is to bring out the discrepancy by inference, that is, instead of seeking to make the witness unsay what he has said, it should be your aim to elicit a statement which may be shown by argument to be inconsistent with the former statement.

" But it must be understood that, in all this, your only purpose should be to ascertain the very truth—to trace an error, if it exists—to try the memory of the witness, if it be trustworthy Never should you seek to entrap him into a falsehood, nor, by your art, to throw him into perplexity, with a design to discredit him, if you believe that not only is he honest, but that he has not erred. Your duty as an advocate is strictly limited by the rules of morality It is no more permissible for you to tamper with the truth in others, or tempt them to confound or conceal it, than to be false yourself. The art to be practised in cross-examination is to be used only when you really believe that the witness has not told the truth, and it is your honest purpose to elicit it

" An explanation is less difficult to be procured from a witness than is a contradiction, because in the case of an explanation the witness has not the fear of being presented in the aspect of one who is perjured. A witness conscious that he has been induced in the examination in chief to say too much, will often seize the opportunity afforded by cross-examination to modify his assertions. If you see this tendency, you have only to encourage it by falling in with his mood, and carefully avoiding anything calculated to make him fear the use to which you may put his admissions. If there be no such tendency, then your course will be the reverse of that to be pursued when you are seeking for contradictions. Instead of avoiding the point, you should go at once to that part of the evidence, repeat the very question, and when you have received the same reply follow it with a series of questions as to the circumstances, which, as you are instructed, go to modify or explain the statements you are combating. If you are satisfied that the witness is honest and truthful, you cannot put your questions too plainly; let them be as leading as you can frame them, naming the fact and in such a form that the answer shall be a plain 'Yes,' or 'No.' And here let us warn you to be cautious not to press your inquiries too far. Having obtained enough for your purpose, pass on. You may obtain too much. There is no more useful faculty in the practice of an advocate than to know when he has done enough. Many more causes are lost by saying too much than by not saying sufficient.

" A chapter may not be uselessly devoted hereafter to the inquiry—*When to sit down?*

2. "The second object of cross-examination is *to elicit something in your favour.* The method of doing this depends upon the character of the witness. If you believe him to be honest and truthful, you may proceed directly to the subject-matter of your inquiry, with plain point-blank questions. But if you suspect that he will not readily state what he is aware will operate in your favour, you must approach him with some of the precautions requisite for the cross-examination of a witness who is not altogether trustworthy. But this distinction in the circumstances is to be observed. Here you are dealing with a witness from whom it is your intent to procure some evidence in your favour. You cannot discredit him, by showing him to be unworthy of belief, without losing the advantage of his testimony on your own behalf. Therefore you cannot venture to probe him by questions that might lead to contradictions. How, then, may you attain your end?

"You can only do so by gradual approaches. The plain direct questions which best elicit the truth from the witness desirous of telling the whole truth and nothing but the truth would, to a witness who desires to suppress some of the truth, operate as a signal for silence. With such a one, the surest course is, by almost imperceptible degrees to conduct him to the end. Elicit one small fact, perhaps but remotely connected with the main object of your inquiry. He may not see the chain of connection, and will answer that question freely, or deem it not worth evading. A very small admission usually requires another to confirm or explain it. Having said so much, the witness cannot stop there, he must go on in self-defence, and thus, by judicious approaches, you bring him to the main point. Even if then he should turn upon you and say no more, you will have done enough to satisfy the jury that his silence is as significant as would have been his confession.

"It may be remarked here that good generalship may be often shown in skilfully availing yourself of *the silence* of a witness. A refusal to answer, or an evasion of your question, will frequently be more serviceable to you than words. On such occasions, when assured of the advantage with which you can employ in your argument to the jury that reluctance to reply, you will not, after having plied him fairly, continue to urge him ; but having done enough to satisfy the Court that he can, if he pleases, say something more, you should withdraw, and then you may suggest such inferences from his silence as may be most advantageous to your cause. It is a frequent and fatal fault of young advocates that they *will have* an answer *in words* to *every* question they put, forgetting that the answer may be injurious, while the silence may be more than suggestive of all that it is their design to elicit.

"The most cautious cross-examination will not always prevent the disagreeable incident of an answer that tells strongly against the questioner. When such a contre-temps occurs to you, do not appear to be taken by surprise. Let neither countenance, nor tone of voice, nor expression of annoyance, show you are conscious of being taken aback. If others exhibit surprise, be you as calm and appear as satisfied as if you had expected the answer in question. Thus you will repel the force of the blow, for, seeing that you are not perplexed by it, the audience may suppose it not to be so important as they deemed it to be, or they give you credit for some profounder purpose than is apparent, or that you are prepared with a contradiction or an explanation. Sometimes, indeed, where the blow has been more than usually staggering, it may not be bad policy to weaken its force by openly making light of it, repeating it, taking a note of it, or appending a joke to it. At no time is self-command more requisite to an advocate than at such a moment, and never is the contrast between experience and inexperience, the prudent and the injudicious, more palpably exhibited.

3 " The *third* object of cross-examination is to discredit the witness, and it will be necessary to preface the hints we venture to offer to you upon the aptest methods of doing this, with a few remarks upon *the principle* that should guide you in the adoption or rejection of this expedient, for it is one upon which there exists somewhat too vague and indefinite an understanding, not merely in the profession, but with the general public, the former erring on the side of laxity, and the latter on that of strictness, the one being influenced by the feelings of an advocate, the other by the sympathies of a witness   Upon so important a matter it must surely be possible to ascertain some rules which may help to determine the limits of an advocate's *duty* in an endeavour to *discredit* a witness by cross-examination. Let us try to trace them.

" In this, as in all other questions of right and wrong, it is necessary to go back beyond the point immediately at issue, to consider the circumstances out of which it

8—2

has arisen. In matters of *duty* and *propriety*, it is most dangerous to introduce refined distinctions, and to seek to justify, by ingenious argument, that which presents itself to the unbiassed and reflecting conscience as wrong. We may fairly doubt the correctness of any proceeding in a matter of morals which needs an argument for its justification. We cannot therefore assent to the conclusions which have been so elaborately wrought out by Lord Brougham and others, as to the duty of an advocate,—conclusions opposed to the plainest dictates of morality, which forbid us to do an injury to our neighbours, or to lie for any purpose whatever, and which are equally binding upon us, whether we are merely acting or speaking for another or upon our own account. We believe sincerely that the character and credit of the profession would be infinitely raised in public esteem if these broad landmarks of morality were more strictly observed in the practice of advocacy, and we are *sure* that in the long run it would be profitable to our clients.

"For if, by arts injurious but wrong, by confusing the honest, browbeating the timid, and putting false constructions upon the words of a witness, a verdict may be stolen now and then, the benefit of such triumphs is more than counterbalanced by the *mistrust* which a departure from candour and fairness, and a resort to arts for concealing or disguising the truth invariably sows in the mind of the Court and of the jury, inclining them to look with suspicion upon everything the unscrupulous advocate says and does, and at length to see in him a trickster always, and to deny to him the credit of frankness and truth-telling, even when he is dealing honestly with them. Who that has addressed juries many times can fail to have seen the incredulous smile that curls upon their lips, and the sort of stern resolve that settles upon their countenance, as if they would say—'We are not going to be bamboozled by you' It is not too much to say, that owing to the reputation which some unscrupulous advocates have earned for the whole body of us, the *prima facie* impression of a jury is almost invariably against the counsel who rises to address them, and that he has to disabuse their minds of this prejudice, by impressing them with his own *truthfulness*, before he can obtain from them a fair consideration of his argument But in justice to our order, it must be admitted that there is now far less cause for this mistrust than there used to be. Advocacy has, in this respect, vastly improved of late years, and is still improving Bullying and brow-beating are as rare now as they were common formerly. It is seldom indeed that unscrupulous assertions and daring misrepresentations of evidence are indulged. The standard of morality has been advanced among us, and is advancing, and it should be your solemn purpose and earnest endeavour not to suffer it to retrograde in your person, but, by beginning with a stern resolve to maintain the loftiest principle of professional virtue, whatever the temptations to the contrary (and they will be many and formidable), to prove by your example that greatness and success as *an advocate* are not only compatible with the strictest integrity as a *man*, but that thenceforward these shall be the only paths to prosperity and honour. When they are seen to bring briefs into the bag, they will not be slow of adoption by those who may have thriven by a different course. Whatever it may once have been, be assured that the day is passing, if it have not passed, when a *tricky* advocate was popular with clients, and one reason of this is, that the law itself has become less *tricky*, a cause depends more upon its merits and less upon quibbles, and therefore its advocate must take a different tone. They will be the most prosperous for the future who see the change and conform themselves to it

"The principle that should govern your conduct in

dealing with an adverse witness, with a view to discredit him, should be that which you would recognise in your private capacity as a Christian gentleman, and which may be summed up in three words—Justice, Truth, Charity. You have no right to tempt, to terrify, or entrap him into falsehood You have no right to charge him with falsehood, unless you are convinced that he is lying, and not that he is merely mistaken. Justice demands that you deal with him as you would be dealt with, were you the witness and he the advocate. Truth demands that you make no endeavour to misrepresent him, or to distort the meaning of his words, contrary to your own conviction of his honesty. Charity demands that you put upon his evidence the construction most accordant with good intentions.

"Only when you are in your own mind thoroughly persuaded that the witness is *not* telling the truth, may you with propriety use your art to entrap him into contradictions, or charge him with falsehood in word or manner. And, indeed, rarely is anything to be gained by such prostitution of the abilities of the advocate as that against which we are warning you. In fact, witnesses do not deliberately lie so frequently as the inexperienced are wont to believe. Downright intended, conscious *perjury*, occurs but seldom.

"But, on the other hand, the same experience will teach you this, which is equally important to be understood, that evidence is far less trustworthy than the public, or jurors who represent the public, suppose it to be In few words, there is much *less* of *perjury*, and vastly *more* of *mistake*, in witnesses, than the unaccustomed observer would imagine to be possible, unless he had studied the physiology of the mind, and had thence learned how manifold are the sources of error, and how imperfect is the sense that conveys the knowledge of facts and the understanding that tries and proves, and applies them.

"To the advocate, however, it is of vital importance that he should attain to the full comprehension of this truth, for it must be the guiding star of his conduct in the cross examination of witnesses. The consciousness of it will govern his words, his voice, his manner; change the tone of mistrust into that of confidence, the language of rebuke into that of kindness; the eye that flashes anger and kindles defiance into the look that wins to frankness.

"Do not let us be misunderstood in the use of the phrase, to discredit a witness. We do not mean by this the vulgar notion of discrediting by making him appear to be perjured. Our meaning is simply to show, by cross-examination, that his evidence is not to be implicitly believed, that he is mistaken in the whole or in parts of it. By adopting this manner of dealing, you not only act in strict accordance with justice, truth, and charity, but you are far more likely to attain your object than by charging wilful falsehood and perjury, by which course, if you fail to impress the jury, you endanger your cause. It not unfrequently happens that a charge of perjury against the witnesses on the other side induces the jury to make the trial a question of the honour of the witnesses instead of the issue on the record. They say, 'If we find for the defendant, after what had been said by his counsel against the plaintiff's witnesses, we shall be confirming his assertion that they are perjured, which we do not believe,' and so, to save the characters of their neighbours whom they believe to be unjustly impugned, they give a verdict against the assailant. Such a result of browbeating and of imputations of perjury and falsehood is by no means rare, and while it affords another instance of the truth of the remark we have already made more than once, that *honesty is wisdom as well as virtue*, it should be treasured in your memory as a warning against a style of cross-examination once popular, but now daily falling more and more

into disrepute, and which is really as bad in policy as it
is discreditable in practice.

" In truth, without imputing perjury, you will find an
ample field for trying the testimony of a witness by
cross-examination and of showing to the jury its weakness
or worthlessness, by bringing into play all that knowledge
of the physiology of mind and of the value of evidence
which it is presumed that you have acquired in your
training for the office of an advocate.   Thus armed, you
will experience no difficulty in applying the various tests
by which the truth is tried, with much more of command
over the witness and vastly more of influence with the
jury, who will always acknowledge the probability of
mistake in a witness, when they will not believe him to
be perjured.   And do not adopt this course as if it were
an art, a contrivance, but frankly and fully, with entire
confidence in its policy as well as its rectitude, so that no
lurking doubt may betray itself in your manner, to throw
a suspicion on your sincerity   It often happens than an
unpractised advocate arms the witness against him,
before he has opened his lips, by a certain defiant look
and air as he rises from his seat as if he were already
revelling in anticipated triumph over his victim.   Nothing
is more fatal than this to success in cross-examination,
for it provokes the pride of the witness, sets him on his
guard, and rouses him to resistance.   He says in his heart,
'You shall get nothing out of me.'   And it is probable
that nothing you will get.

" A sober quietness, an expression of good temper, a
certain friendliness of look and manner, which will be
understood, although it cannot be described, should
distinguish you when you commence the cross-examination of a witness, the truth of whose testimony you are
going to try, not by the vulgar arts of browbeating,
misrepresenting, insulting, and frightening into contradictions, but by the more fair, more honourable, and more
successful, if more difficult, method of showing him to be

mistaken. You must begin with conciliation; you must remove the fear which the most truthful witness feels when about to be subjected to the ordeal of cross-examination Let him understand, as soon as possible that you are not about to insult him nor to entrap him into falsehood nor to take unfair advantages of him; that you have confidence in his desire to tell the truth, and all the truth, and that your object is to ascertain the precise limits of truth in the story he has told

"Proceed very gently, and only, as it were, with the fringe of the case, until you see that the witness is reassured, and that a good understanding has been established between you, to which a smiling question that elicits a smiling answer will be found materially to contribute. A witness who stubbornly resists every other advance on the part of the advocate will often yield at once to a good-humoured remark that compels the lips to curl. This point gained, you may at once proceed to your object.

"The other purposes of cross-examination have been previously explained. We are now considering only what is to be done when the design is to discredit the testimony, not by discrediting the witness, but by showing that he is mistaken; that he has been himself deceived. Now, the way to do this is by closely inquiring into the sources of his knowledge; and here it is that so much analytical skill, so intimate an acquaintance with mind and its operations, is demanded on your part, and that you should avert resistance to your inquiries on the part of the witness.

"Perhaps it is unnecessary to inform you that it is useless to put to a witness directly the question, if he is sure that the fact was as he has stated it. He will only be the more positive. No witness will ever admit that he could have been mistaken. This is shown remarkably in cases where personal identity is in question. Everybody admits that there is nothing upon which all persons are so often mistaken, yet, is there nothing upon which witnesses are more positive, and that positiveness is continually influencing inconsiderate juries to erroneous verdicts, as the records of our criminal law painfully prove, for of the wrongful convictions, fully one half have been cases of mistaken identity, in which witnesses have been too positive, and juries too confiding, in a matter which their own daily experience should satisfy them to be, of all others, the most dubious and unsatisfactory Instead, therefore, of asking the witness whether he might not be mistaken, you should proceed at once to discover the probabilities of mistake, by tracing the sources of his knowledge, and by eliciting all the circumstances, internal and external, under which it was formed. It is in this operation that the faculties of the skilful advocate are displayed, this it is that calls into play his acquaintance with mental physiology, his experience of men and things, and in which he exhibits his superiority over the imperfectly educated and the inexperienced.

"By what process do you perform this difficult duty, and achieve this triumph of your art? Let us endeavour to describe it.

"The witness has detailed an occurrence at a certain time and place, and it is your purpose to show that he was mistaken in some of the particulars, and that the inferences he drew from them were incorrect, or not justified by the facts. Your first proceeding to this end is to realise the scene in your own mind. Your fancy must paint for you a picture of the place, the persons, the accessories. You then ask the witness to repeat the story, you note its congruity or otherwise with the circumstances that accompanied it, you detect improbabilities or impossibilities. You see as he saw, and you learn in what particulars he saw imperfectly, and how he formed too hasty conclusions; how prejudice may have influenced him; how things dimly seen were by the imagination transformed into other things in his memory.

"How erring the senses are, and how much their impressions are afterward moulded by the mind, how very fallible is information seemingly the most assured, it needs no extensive observation to teach. If you make inquiry as to an occurrence in the next street, ten minutes after it has happened, and from half-a-dozen actual spectators of it, you will receive as many different accounts of its details, and yet each one positive as to the truth of his own narrative, and the error of his neighbours It is so with all testimony, and hence, whatever depends upon the senses or the memory of a witness, however honest and truth-speaking he may be in intention, is fairly open to doubt, to question, to investigation, and to denial, for the purpose of showing that it ought not to be relied upon, and that it may have, upon the question under consideration, a bearing altogether different from that for which it was employed by the party who adduced it

"But it is not enough to ascertain that the witness is mistaken, to satisfy the jury, when you come to comment upon his evidence, you must learn whence the mistake arose, and you should not leave him until you have attained your object Sometimes you may procure this from the witness's mouth thus —Having gathered from his description that, in the circumstances of place or time, or otherwise, as the case may be, it was impossible or improbable that he could have seen or heard enough to justify his positive conclusion, you plainly put to him the question, how it is that, being so situated, he could have so seen or heard This will usually elicit an explanation that will at once be a confession of his mistake and a discovery of the cause of it.

"Caution is nevertheless necessary in this proceeding, and it should be resorted to only when other means have

failed ; for, having ascertained to your own satisfaction
the mistakes of the witness and the facts that prove
them to be mistakes, the exhibition of them will come
with far better effect in your address to the jury, when
lucidly displayed in argument, than when evolved bit by
bit in the course of a long examination   Usually, it
will be sufficient for you that you have the fact   Besides,
it is well that the witness himself is not made conscious
of detected error, lest, fearing to have his veracity
impugned, he should close his mind against you, and
resist further investigation into the parts of his story
which yet remain to be tried.

"The art of cross-examination, however, is not limited
to the detection of mistakes in a witness.   Sometimes it
happens that you have good reason to believe that he is
not mistaken, but that he is lying ; and when you are
assured of this, but not otherwise, you may treat him as
a liar and deal with him accordingly.   Your object will
now be to prove him to be a liar out of his own mouth,
and it will be permissible to resort to many a stratagem
for the purpose of detection which may not be fairly
used towards a witness whom you believe to be honest
but mistaken

"The question has often occurred to us whether it is
more prudent to show such a witness that you suspect
him, or to conceal your doubts of his honesty.   Either
course has its advantages.   By displaying your doubts
you incur the risk of setting him upon his guard, and
leading him to be more positive in his assertions and
more circumspect in his answers, but, on the other hand,
a conscious liar is almost always a moral coward ; when
he sees that he is detected, he can rarely muster courage
to do more than reiterate his assertion ; he has not the
presence of mind to carry out the story by ingenious
invention of details, and a consistent narrative of
accidental circumstances connected with it.   A cautious
concealment of your suspicions possesses the advantage

of enabling you to conduct him into a labyrinth before he is aware of your design, and so to expose his falsehood by self-contradiction and absurdities. Perhaps either course might be adopted, according to the character of the witness. If he is a cool, shrewd fellow, it may be more prudent to conceal from him your doubts of his veracity until he has furnished you with the proof. If he is one of that numerous class who have merely got up a story to which they doggedly adhere, it may be wise to awe him at once by notice that you do not believe him, and that you do not intend to spare him We have often seen such a witness surrender at discretion on the first intimation of such an ordeal. This is one of the arts of advocacy which cannot be taught by anything but experience. It is to be learned only by the language of the eye, the countenance, the tones of the voice, that betray to the practised observer what is passing in the mind within.

" But having, after a glance at your man, resolved upon your course, pursue it resolutely. Be not deterred by finding your attacks parried at first Persevere until you have obtained your object, or are convinced that your impression was wrong, and that the witness is telling the truth. If you determine to adopt the course of hiding from him your doubts, be careful not to betray doubt by your face, nor by tone of voice. A good advocate is a good actor, and it is one of the faculties of an actor to command his countenance. Open gently, mildly ; do not appear to doubt the witness ; go at once to the marrow of the story he has told, as if you were not afraid of it , make him repeat it , then carry him away to some distant and collateral topic and try his memory upon that, so as to divert his thoughts from the main object of your inquiry, and prevent his seeing the connection between the tale he has told and the question you are about to put to him Then, by slow approaches, bring him back to the main circumstances, by the investigation of which it is that you purpose to show the falsity of the story

"The design of this manœuvre is, of course, to prevent him from seeing the connection between his own story and your examination, so that he may not draw upon his imagination for explanations consistent with his original evidence; your design being to elicit inconsistency and contradictions between the story itself and other circumstances, from which it may be concluded that it is a fabrication.

"As a specimen of the sort of cross-examination to which we refer ·   In case of affiliation of a bastard child, the mother had sworn distinctly and positively to the person of the father, and to the time and place of their acquaintance, fixed, as usual, at precisely the proper period before the birth of the child   In this case, the time sworn to was the middle of May; and the place, the putative father's garden; for an hour the witness endured the strictest cross-examination that ingenuity could suggest, she was not to be shaken in any material part of the story, she had learned it well, and with the persistence that makes women such difficult witnesses to defeat, she adhered to it.   She was not to be thrown off her guard by a question for which she was not prepared, and the examination proceeded thus:—'You say you walked in the garden with Mr. M——? Yes. Before your connection with him ? Yes.   More than once?   Yes; several times.   Did you do so afterwards ? No.   Never once?   No   Is there fruit in the garden ? Yes.   I suppose you were not allowed to pick any ? Oh, yes; he used to give me some.   What fruit ? Currants and raspberries   Ripe ?   Yes.'

"This was enough.   She was detected at once.   The alleged intercourse was in the middle of May.   Currants and raspberries are not ripe till June.   In this case the woman's whole story was untrue   She had fallen in with the suggestion about fruit to strengthen, as she thought, her account of the garden. But she did not perceive the drift of the questions, and consequently had not sufficient self-command to reflect that the fruit named was not ripe in May.

"This will serve as an illustration of the manner in which the most acute witness may be detected in a lie. But patience in the pursuit is always necessary. You may be baffled once and again, but be careful never to let it be seen that you are baffled. Glide quietly into another track, and try another approach; you can scarcely fail of success at last. No false witness is armed at all points.

"But, in the process—somewhat tedious, it is true, to yourself, and not always comprehended by others—the art of the witness will not be the only nor the severest trial of your temper. Too often you will find the Judge complaining of the tediousness of repetition He does not always see your drift, and especially, if you are young, he is apt to conclude that you are putting questions at random, and to refuse you credit for a meaning and a design in your queries. You must, in such case, firmly but respectfully assert your right to conduct your examination after your own fashion, and proceed, without perturbation, in the path your deliberate judgment has prescribed. Your duty is to your client, and you must discharge it fearlessly, leaving to the event and to experience to vindicate your motives and prove the wisdom of your conduct After a while the Judge will discover that you do not act without a sufficient reason, and that you have a design in your cross-examination. It must, however, be confessed that cross-examination is so often conducted at random, without aim, or plan, or purpose, as if for the mere sake of saying something, that Judges may well be excused for suspecting a divergent course in a junior, and attributing to inexperience a string of questions which are in fact the result of profound deliberation and design.

"If, however, you adopt the other course, and, instead of surprising the witness into the betrayal of his falsehood, you resolve to bring it out of him by a bold and open attack—to awe him, as it were, into honesty—aspect and voice must express your consciousness of his perjury, and your resolve to have the truth. A stern, determined fixing of your eye upon his, will often suffice to unnerve him, and will certainly help you to assure yourself whether your suspicions are just or unjust. It may be stated, as a general rule, that a witness who is lying will not look you fully in the face with a steady gaze, his eye quivers and turns away, is cast down, and wanders restlessly about. On the contrary, the witness who is speaking the truth, or what he believes to be the truth, will meet your gaze, however timidly, will look at you when he answers your questions, and will let you look into his eyes. There may be exceptions to this rule, but it rarely fails to inform the advocate whether the person subject to cross examination is the witness of truth or of falsehood

" Thus assured, and pursuing your plan of bold attack, there needs to be no circumlocution, no gradual approaching, as in the other method of surprisal, but go straightway to your object, plunging the witness at once into the story you are questioning. Make him repeat it slowly. It will often be that, under the discomposure of your detection of his purpose, he will directly vary from his former statement, and if he does so in material points, which are sufficient to discredit him, it will usually be the more prudent course to leave him there, self-condemned, instead of continuing the examination, lest you should give him time to rally, and perhaps contrive a story that will explain away his contradictions. If, however, his lesson is well learned, and he repeats the narrative very nearly as at first, you will have to try another course, which will tax your ingenuity and patience.

" Procure from him in detail, and let his words be taken down, the particulars of his story, and then question him as to associated circumstances as to which he is not likely to have prepared himself, and to answer which, therefore, he must draw on his invention at the instant Some ingenuity will be necessary on your part, after surveying his story, to select the weakest points for your experiment, and to suggest the circumstances least likely to have been pre-arranged Having obtained his answers, permit him no pause, but instantly take him to a new subject, lead his thoughts away altogether from the matter of your main topic. The more irrelevant your queries the better, your purpose is to occupy his mind with a new train of ideas. Conduct him to different places and persons and events. Then, as suddenly, in the very midst of your questionings, when his mind is the most remote from the subject, when he is expecting the next question to relate to the one that has gone before, suddenly return to your first point, not repeating the main story, for this, having been well learned, will probably be repeated as before, but to those circumstances associated with it upon which you had surprised him into invention on the moment. It is probable that, after such a diversion of his thoughts, he will have forgotten what his answers were, what were the fictions with which he had filled up the accessories of his false narrative, and having no leisure allowed to him for reflection, he will now give a different account of them, and so betray his falsehood Of all the arts of cross-examination, there are none so efficient as this for the detection of a lie.

" Another excellent plan is to take the witness through his story but not in the same order of incidents in which he told it. Dislocate his train of ideas, and you put him out; you disturb his memory of his lesson. Thus begin your cross-examination at the middle of his narrative, then jump to one end, then to some other part the most

W.C.   9

remote from the subject of the previous question   If he
is telling the truth, this will not confuse him, because he
speaks from impressions upon his mind ; but if he is
lying, he will be perplexed and will betray himself, for
speaking from the memory only, which acts by association, you disturb that association, and his invention
breaks down

"When you are satisfied that the witness is drawing
upon his invention, there is no more certain process of
detection than a rapid fire of questions   Give him no
pause between them ; no breathing place, nor point to
rally. Few minds are sufficiently self-possessed as, under
such a catechising, to maintain a consistent story. If
there be a pause or a hesitation in the answer, you
thereby lay bare the falsehood   The witness is conscious
that he dares not to stop to think whether the answer he
is about to give will be consistent with the answers
already given, and he is betrayed by his contradictions.
In this process it is necessary to fix him to time, and
place, and names. 'You heard him say so?' 'When?'
'Where ?'   'Who was present?'   'Name   them'
'Name one of them'   Such a string of questions,
following one upon the other as fast as the answer is
given, will frequently confound the most audacious   Fit
names, and times and places, are not readily invented,
or if invented, not readily remembered. Nor does the
objection apply to this that may undoubtedly be urged
against some others of the arts by which an advocate
detects falsehood, namely, that it is liable to perplex the
innocent, as well as to confound the guilty; for if the
tale be true, the answers to such questions present
themselves instantaneously to the witness's lips   They
are so associated in his mind with the main fact to which
he is speaking, that it is impossible to recall the one
without the other. Collateral circumstances may be
forgotten by the most truthful, or even be unobserved ;
but time, place, and audience are a part of the

transaction, without which memory of the fact itself can scarcely exist.

" There is no branch of our subject on which a wider difference of opinion prevails than upon the weight to be given to variations by a witness in the telling of a story—counsel usually dwelling upon them as evidence of falsehood, and Judges almost always directing the jury that they are rather evidences of honesty. As these views are often sincerely entertained by both, and considerable practical inconvenience results from so wide a difference, it may be useful, in this place, to endeavour to reconcile these opposite conclusions of intelligent minds, as only they can be reconciled, by reference to *principles*

" Memory is association, ideas return linked together as they were originally presented to the mind, and the presence of one summons the other by suggestion An event is witnessed, and the scene and its accessories are impressed upon the mind. But it is only impressed there as the spectator beheld it, and not necessarily as it was in reality. It is necessary to ascertain also the medium through which he saw or heard, before we can properly estimate the value of his memory. When called upon to bear testimony to the fact, if he desires to tell the truth, he will describe, as nearly as he can in words, so much as he can recall of the circumstances. But it by no means follows that, every time he recalls the scene, it should present itself to his mind in precisely the same aspect, and for this reason, the mind does not revive the whole at once, but in succession, and some portions of it will come back more vividly at one time than at another, and, by their very vividness, recall other associations before unremembered. Hence, differences in description, and especially new circumstances intro- duced into a repeated narrative, although each repetition should vary from all the former ones, by the addition of some things and the omission of others, do not afford

9—2

the slightest grounds for imputing perjury to a witness; on the contrary, they are rather a presumption in his favour, for an invention that is learned would probably be recalled as it was learned, with the same facts, and almost in the same words.

"But it is otherwise with discrepancies of statement. These cannot exist in a truthful narrative. Repeated never so frequently and whatever the variance in detail, the story will always be consistent with itself, and with its former assertions. A positive discrepancy is proof that whatever the cause, whether by design or by the not unfrequent delusion of mistaking imagination for reality, the witness is not speaking the truth, and therefore in such a case, be the motive what it may, an advocate is justified in pointing out this discrepancy to the jury, and asserting that no faith can be placed in a narrative which thus contains within itself decisive evidence that some portion of it, at least, is not true. By bearing in mind the distinction between variances and discrepancies in the repetitions by a witness in the same story, the Judge and the advocate may avoid those contradictions of assertion as to the worth of certain testimony which sometimes shake the confidence of juries in arguments really deserving their consideration and which are equally disagreeable to the speaker and to the commentator. Let the advocate abstain from dwelling upon mere variances, and let the Judge, before he directs the jury the advocate is wrong in his assertions, as cautiously assure himself that the objections that have been urged are not to discrepancies but to differences.

"We have already noticed the difficulty sometimes experienced by an advocate from the impatience of the Judge at repetitions of the same questions. Too often he is met with the remark, 'Mr. ——, you have asked that question before,' or, 'The witness has already told you.' This is doubly disagreeable, for besides putting you on ill terms with the Court, it disturbs your plans, and sets the witness on his guard. There is nothing of which the Bench is so little tolerant as of the repetition of the same question, and yet there are few more effective methods of detecting a falsehood. The witness answers. You note his answer. You pass away to some distant part of the story, or some foreign transaction. You then on a sudden return, when his thoughts have been otherwise engaged, when probably he has forgotten his first answer, if it was false, and you obtain a different one, which instantly betrays him Often we have seen witnesses proof against all other tests fail before this one When your design is distinctly this, and not merely a vague, purposeless interrogation, proceed respectfully but firmly to show that you have a meaning, and your aims will soon come to be understood and respected by the Court.

"Be careful to avoid contracting a habit into which an advocate is liable to lapse if he does not keep guard over himself at the beginning of his practice. Do not indulge too much in adjurations to witnesses to speak the truth, reminding them continually that they are on their oaths, as, 'Now, sir, upon your solemn oath,' 'Remember, you are upon oath, and take care what you say,' and such like. If frequently introduced, they lose their force by repetition. They are very effective when judiciously employed, and uttered with due solemnity of tone and manner, and on fit occasions; but they should not be put forward on every slight pretence as well to frighten an honest as to awe a dishonest witness Reserve such an appeal for times when it may be used with effect, because with obvious propriety. When you believe that a witness is tampering with his conscience you may sometimes successfully prevent the contemplated perjury by a solemn appeal, and especially if you add to it an exhortation not to be hasty in his answer, but to think before he speaks. The countenance, the tone of the voice, the very attitude, should express the language you utter   You may word it somewhat after this fashion · ' Remember, you have sworn to tell the truth and the whole truth.   Now (put the question, and add), think before you speak, and answer me truly as you have called God to witness your words'   It is one of the faults common to young advocates that they make too free a use of this appeal to witnesses, wasting its worth by familiarity; hence, as with all familiar things, the tone and manner that gave it power are lost, and failure is the result.

"Sometimes a witness will not answer.   He does not choose to know.   He will not remember   He is obstinately ignorant.   You are aware that he could tell you a great deal if he pleased, but he has reasons for forgetting Such a witness will task your skill and patience.   To conquer him you will need as much of patience as of art.   The first rule is, to keep your temper, the second, to be as resolute as himself, the third, to discover his weak place—every person has some weak point, through which he is accessible.   If you betray the slightest want of temper, the witness will have the advantage of you, for you will enlist his pride in defence of his determination.   If you show him that you are resolved to have an answer, you will shake him by the influence which a strong will always obtains over a weaker one, and by that wonderful power which persistency never fails to exercise   To find out his weaknesses, you must peruse his character by the art which it is assumed you have cultivated, of reading the mind in the face.   Then work him accordingly.   The surest method is the smiling and jocose   Many a man who will withstand unmoved a torrent of abuse, or rather become more obstinate under its influence, will surrender to a smiling face and good-humoured joke.   If this fail, there yet remains another resource, more difficult of appliance, and demanding the most consummate mastery of the art of cross-examination.

You must now approach him by stratagem. Your object is to procure him to admit so much that he cannot help telling you the whole story. The difficulty of this consists in the extreme caution required to approach him so that your object shall not be perceptible to him; so to frame your questions that he shall not see the connection between the answer he is about to give and the confession you desire to abstract from him In appearance the questions must be dissevered from the immediate subject sought, but in fact, they must be associated with it The approach must be so gradually made as not to excite suspicion, and perhaps it is well to open with something quite foreign to the subject-matter Having obtained an answer, you put another query that appears naturally to follow from the former and so on, until you link with the question something that is associated with the matter sought for. It is not easy for a witness to discover the links of such a chain, and he is sure to make some admission that will negative his alleged ignorance of the transaction, and compel him, having yielded so much, to surrender the whole Taking, then, this maxim for your guidance, that, whatever sophistry may suggest to the contrary, you have *no right* to attempt to discredit a witness by perplexing him into contradictions, unless you entertain the strongest suspicion that he is not telling the truth, or the whole truth, let us now proceed to consider what kind of con-tradiction is requisite to such a conclusion, for upon this there is evidently much misunderstanding among inex-perienced advocates. Remember that your object is to convince the Judge and jury that the witness is unworthy of credit. In answer to the questions of his own counsel in the examination in chief he has told an apparently straightforward and consistent story He could scarcely do otherwise. He had previously made his statement to the attorney; it had been taken down and read to him, perhaps more than once, he has had leisure to supply whatever was defective, or to clear up whatever was obscure. His cautious counsel has also employed his ingenuity in the avoidance of any questions that might mar the completeness of the narrative. If you reasonably suspect that the story is forged or coloured, or only partially told, it will be your duty to discover and display its defects   If you believe it to be a false-hood or misrepresentation, it will be your endeavour to make him contradict himself.   If you believe that there is a *suppressio veri*, your ingenuity will be exerted to extract the truth that has been withheld

"Beware that you do not fall into the fault, only too common with the inexperienced, of seizing upon small and unimportant discrepancies.   Experience teaches us that there are few who can tell the same story twice in precisely the same way, but they will add or omit some-thing, and even vary in the description of minute particulars.   Indeed, a verbatim recital of the same tale by a witness is usually taken as proof that he is repeating a lesson rather than narrating facts seen.   A discrepancy, to be of any value in discrediting a witness, must be in some particular which, according to common experience, a man is not likely to have observed so slightly as that he would give two different descriptions of it   Remember that you are dealing with a jury composed of men who cannot understand refined distinctions, and have no respect for petty artifices and small triumphs over a witness's self-possession or memory, and that you will not win their verdict unless you show that the witness is not puzzled, but lying.   Yet how often may this error be seen in our Courts, and verdicts lost by the very cunning that was pluming itself upon its ingenuity.

"When a witness, upon his examination in chief, anticipates the counsel, and, instead of waiting to be questioned, or after two or three questions have been put to him, proceeds to tell his whole story, and will go on in spite of every effort made to stop him, observe him closely, to ascertain from his manner whether he is telling the truth, or merely repeating a lesson learned by heart.

"It is wrong to suppose, as some do, that when a witness thus dispenses with questions and pours out his whole story in a continuous stream, he is therefore always lying. It is not so. There are many minds in which the association of ideas is so fragile, that if the thread is once snapped, they cannot, without great difficulty, take it up again at the place where it was broken; they must begin at the beginning and go right through every incident as it occurred, however trivial or irrelevant to the main story, conscious of this defect, and once set agoing, they have an irresistible impulse to proceed without pause until they have delivered themselves of all they have to say. Such a witness, it is obvious, is not only not to be discredited, but his testimony is of more real worth than that of a more passive witness, because the very structure of mind that prevents him from taking up the thread of a story at any point, and the memory that can only be revived by the recalling of every circumstance in the precise order of its occurrence, forbids the introduction of fictions which would necessarily destroy the entire chain, and plunge his mind into chaos.

"Your care will be to distinguish between the witness who from this cause runs through his story, and the witness who does so because he is repeating a lesson learned by rote. Close observation will enable you to discover a difference in the look, the tone, the manner, and the language. When relating what he has *seen*, there is always an aspect of intelligence, even in the dullest, the eye kindles, the face brightens, the expression changes with the incidents narrated. Still more does the tone of the voice reveal the speaker's truth, its changes are dramatic; it varies with every emotion that flashes across the mind, awakened by the recalling of the incidents described   The *manner* is usually eager and energetic, and in strict accordance with the tones, the aspect, and the theme.   And even if these signs should be wanting you must not, therefore, decide against the veracity of the witness until you have considered his *language*.   If he is honest, his language will always be such as is consistent with his condition of life—appropriate to age, sex, education, and calling.   Moreover, it will exhibit that fitness for the subject without preference to structure of sentences which always distinguishes extempore narrative.   If these characteristics, or either of them, be present, you may safely assume that the witness is telling the truth, but that he is only able to do so after his own fashion of a continuous story, and cannot recall it by scraps, under interrogation.

"If, on the other hand, he is repeating by rote a lesson which he has committed to memory, you will find wanting in him all or most of the signs of truth above described.   He stands quite still, excepting, it may be, an uneasy motion of the hands or feet.   His face has no meaning in it.   His eyes are fixed—not upon the counsel, the Judge, or the jury, but upon the wall, or more commonly turned upwards, with a sort of vacant stare. His voice is monotonous, and expresses no emotion.   His delivery is rapid, unless when seized by a sudden forgetfulness, when he makes a full stop, or after stumbling a little tries back again, in hopes to regain the last word or thought   His language, also, is almost always inappropriate to his position, for in such case it would seldom be his own composition that he has learned, but something which another has put into words, which words would not be those of the pupil, but of the master.   A single expression will often suffice to betray to you this sort of *taught testimony*, when it is one which you know such a person as the witness would not have used, and perhaps there is no test so difficult to evade, and so conclusive where it prevails, as this of *language*.   The reason is plain. A witness learns his lesson thus : He tells what he knows to the attorney or his clerk. If they be of the unscrupulous class, which has happily become so rare, the witness is informed that his evidence is of no use, but that if he had known so-and-so, he would have been taken to the assizes. The hint suffices. The memory is racked again, and the testimony desired is *then* found. It is taken down in writing His entire story is put into formal shape ; it is read over to him again and again, until he has it almost by heart. He learns, not merely the facts he is to prove, but the very words in which those words are narrated in the brief, and he repeats them as he has learned them.

"Having thus satisfied yourself of the fact that he is lying, you may, in your cross-examination, endeavour to discredit the witness with the jury. Your attack may be most successfully conducted thus Without previous questioning come at once to the point, and ask him to repeat his account of the transaction He will do so in almost the self-same words with the same aspect and manner, and in the same tone and language, before and after the episode So certain is this that, if it fails, you may fairly suppose that whatever other objections may be offered to the testimony, it is not a story repeated by rote. The recent alteration in the law of evidence, not only permitting but compelling the examination of the parties to a suit, calls for some observations before we can conclude the subject of cross-examination, for it will probably require of the advocate a special direction of his faculties. This wise measure was for a long time successfully resisted, on the plea that, so great was the interest of parties, and such, therefore, the temptation to falsehood, no reliance could be placed on their testimony To this the answer was, that the security of Judges and juries in the reception of evidence is not so much dependent on the oath taken by the witness to speak the truth as upon the sifting to which the evidence is subjected by cross-examination, that it is unjust to exclude *all* parties to suits because some might not be trustworthy, and that some persons who were deemed competent to try the value of all other testimony were equally competent to try that of the parties, whom, because of their interest, they would necessarily watch with the greater strictness, and receive with the more caution. This argument at length prevailed, and the witness-box is now open to all, leaving it to the sagacity of counsel and the discretion of the Court to determine, from the demeanour of the witness, the intrinsic probability of his story, the manner in which he endures a cross-examination, and the other tests by which truth is distinguished from falsehood, whether he is worthy of credit, and to what extent. Thus will a new duty devolve upon the advocate for the future in the examination and cross-examination of the parties.

" In the examination in chief you need observe no difference of conduct towards a party to the suit and any other witness, excepting, perhaps, a little care to rein him in if he should appear to be too eager. But, in cross-examination, you must take into account the fact that a party has a strong bias of interest which may tempt him to tell a deliberate lie, but which is much more likely to colour his impressions, and produce self-deception So that he may have the most confident belief in the truth of that which he is stating, and yet it may be false in fact. Therefore, where a party to the suit is a witness, you should subject him to the most rigid cross-examination, to test his accuracy. The manner of doing this will vary somewhat from that which has been suggested as applicable to other classes of witnesses

" You may assume the existence of a strong prejudice and bias, but not, therefore, necessarily of an intention to deceive. Great caution will be required in dealing with him. You will have occasion to employ by turns all the tests of truth that have been already described. You will soon discover from the manner of the witness if he means well, if he is scrupulous, or if he is blinded by his feelings, or deliberately determined, at any cost of veracity, to advance his own cause. His countenance, his tone, his manner of answering the questions put to him, will sufficiently reveal his character.

"If he is manifestly desirous of speaking the truth, your course is clear. Let him see that such is your opinion of him. Encourage his honest intents by frank acknowledgments. If the examination in chief has brought out only a portion of the facts, it will be your business to supply the deficiencies and elicit the whole story. No ingenuity will be required for this with such a witness. You may advance directly to your object He will give straightforward answers to your questions, and the more plain they are the more ready and full will be his replies. But such a witness is the most dangerous one to you The same honesty which enables to obtain a ready answer to your questions, and to elicit every circumstance connected with the transaction, will carry conviction to the jury also, and his testimony will be received with unhesitating confidence. If, therefore, you do not expect to obtain from him some facts which may weaken your opponent's case, it will be more prudent not to cross-examine him at all, or only to put a few questions that have no bearing on the case merely that you may not appear to have abandoned your cause The more truthful he is, the more likely it is that every answer you will obtain will make his case the stronger, and damage your case the more. Before you begin your cross-examination, ascertain from your attorney if there is really any probability of *explaining away* the facts proved by the witness. If that is hopeless your wisest course will be to take the chance of *omissions* in the examination in chief which are always more or less to be found by reason of the fear which a cautious counsel has of putting questions that may elicit unfavourable replies and so to trust to your ingenuity to make the most of *them* in your address to the jury. At all events, a cross-examination is more likely to injure than to help you.

"But if you see that the witness is biassed, you must employ some artifice. Direct questions will not suffice You must approach him with caution, and indirectly. Begin by giving him credit for good intentions. Do not appear to mistrust him. Flatter him even with the assurance that you believe he desires to tell the whole truth. It is a great point to have him pleased with himself, for your purpose is, not only to unveil him to others, but to strip from his own eyes the veil of self-deception so that his vanity will not be enlisted against you. Remind him, by your first question, that he is a party to the cause, and has the strongest interest in the result. Follow it with the assurance of your own confidence, that, in spite of this bias, he desires to tell the whole truth ; but, although he has no intent to deceive, the truth is not as he has stated ; blinded by his feelings or his interests, he has seen the truth only partially, or distorted, or falsely coloured. Your duty is either to elicit the very truth as it was or to show that, being thus self-deceived, his testimony is not to be relied upon. How may you best do this ? Remember the position of the witness. He has impressions upon his mind which he *believes* to be *true*. He, therefore, unhesitatingly swears to them as facts It is obvious that direct questioning will fail to effect this, for to a mere repetition of the question as to what he saw or heard, the same answer as before will be given. Again he tells you what was his impression of the fact, and it is all that he can tell you ; it is all in truth which any of us can tell, for with every man, knowledge is only of the impressions of his own mind, and not of *the very fact itself*, which may present itself to many minds in many different aspects. The only means of shaking such testimony is to show it to be inconsistent with other facts, or with those strong probabilities arising out of the usual order of things, the ready perception of which constitutes what is called common sense. It is in eliciting this inconsistency either with the rest of the story, or with the common sense of mankind, of which a jury is generally a pretty fair representative, that the skill and ingenuity, aided by the experience, of an advocate is demanded.

"There is no difference in this respect in the cross-examination of a party, and that of any other interested witness. In both instances the process will be the same, to approach him by indirect and not by direct questions, and to employ all your efforts to elicit contradictions and inconsistencies between the facts positively asserted by the witness and other undoubted facts, or between his testimony and probability and common sense, from which you may argue that no reliance can be placed upon the evidence, not because the witness has been guilty of perjury, or intends to deceive, but because he has fallen into error This is an argument which rarely fails to convince, because it is in accordance with experience, and is infinitely more effective than one which imputes every mistake or mis-statement to deliberate perjury.

"In dealing with a party to the suit as a witness, you have this advantage, that his testimony will be watched with more strictness and subjected to a severer scrutiny, than would the evidence of an unbiassed witness. If the advocate is satisfied that the witness is lying he should involve him in a maze of contradictions, which it is almost impossible for the most skilful liar to avoid, because the quickest mind cannot in a moment calculate the effect of its present answer upon the past, or anticipate the bearing of the reply it is about to give upon the questions that are to follow. Hence it is that cross-examination has always been deemed the surest test of truth, and a better security than the oath.

"The witness has already echoed the questions of his own counsel, and proved his own case, and being well prepared with that he will of course repeat the lesson he has learned, without alteration or hesitation, and the more positively the more you press him, therefore it is a waste of time and helping him more than yourself to repeat those self-same questions   Yet how often is this done.   With a slight alteration of phrase and an attempt to be stern, counsel sometimes persist in repeating the very question which the witness has already distinctly answered.   'Do you mean to tell the jury upon your oath that you heard him say so?' 'Will you swear that you saw Smith strike him?' and such like; to which the answer is, 'I have said so already,' 'I have sworn it.'   No other answer could be expected.   The witness had come prepared to prove these very facts, and, although false, having once sworn to them he cannot do otherwise than re-state them, however frequently the question may be repeated.   This manner of proceeding is, therefore, worse than worthless, and you will at once direct your efforts to the eliciting of contradictions, by which we do not mean trifling differences of phrase, or discrepancies in small matters, which the witness is not likely to have observed very accurately, and on which, therefore, his story might vary upon every repetition, without any intentional falsehood, but unquestionable contradictions or statements, so obvious that the witness could not have believed both to be true.   If he is lying, no presence of mind or ingenuity will enable him to escape from your pursuit, provided you conduct it with proper skill, giving him no time for reflection, and so engaging his attention that he shall not have leisure to digest his answers, or to see how they square with the story he has already told

"The principle of this manner of cross-examination is,

that truth is always consistent with itself. If the witness is telling the truth, his answers will be in substantial accordance with the story he has already told, and with any questions that may be put to him. He has no need to consider their bearing, and therefore his reply is as prompt as memory. On the contrary, a witness who is telling a false story can rarely so construct it that it shall be consistent with other associated circumstances which it is impossible to anticipate

"Hence it is that you must try the witness by questions on matters which only bear indirectly upon the point at issue. As for instance, if he has sworn that on a certain day a certain person made to him a certain statement You cannot directly shake the fact thus sworn to, for the witness has but to adhere to his assertion and he will baffle any amount of direct interrogation. But it is not at all likely that he has prepared himself with all the accompanying particulars, therefore you put such questions as these · Where was the conversation held? At what time of the day? Who was present? Were they sitting or standing? How did he come to the place? Whom did he meet on the way? How was he dressed— and the other party? Did they speak loud or low? Did they eat or drink together, and what? Did anybody come in while they were talking? How long were they together? When they parted which way did each take? Whom did he meet afterward? At what time did he reach his home? and so forth, as the particular circumstances of the case may suggest, but always, if possible, preferring facts spoken to by other witnesses, so that you may expose him, not only by his self-contradictions, but by the testimony of others. When questions of this kind are rapidly pushed, they deprive the false witness of opportunity to fit them to his previous story. You should also carefully avoid putting them in any natural sequence of time or place, for that is to suggest to him a story which he will invent quite as rapidly as you can construct your questions. Dislocate them as much as possible. Take now one part of the story, then another. Dodge him backward and forward, from one object to the other, so that it shall be impossible for him to be prepared by one question for the next, or that one answer shall be the prompter of its successor. The difficulty of doing this well is very great, and therefore, perhaps, it is that it is so rarely seen to be well done ; but it is an accomplishment, wanting which, the advocate is not a master of his art.

"There is one kind of testimony which will sometimes baffle the utmost skill. It is the case of a witness who swears positively to some single fact, occurring when no other person was present, or but one, now dead or far distant, whom, therefore, it is impossible to contradict, and equally difficult to involve in self-contradiction, because all the circumstances may be true, except the one which he has been called to prove.

"In such a case there remains only an appeal to the jury or Judge to look with suspicion upon evidence so easily forged, so impossible to be disproved, and ask that its worth be tried by its intrinsic probabilities, showing, if you can, how improbable it is that such a statement should have been so made, or such a circumstance have occurred.

"In concluding these remarks on cross-examination, the rarest, the most useful, and the most difficult to be acquired of the accomplishments of the advocate, we would again urge upon your attention the importance of calm discretion. In addressing a jury you may sometimes talk without having anything to say, and no harm will come of it. But in cross-examination every question that does not advance your cause injures it. If you have not a definite object to attain, dismiss the witness without a word. There are no harmless questions here ; the most apparently unimportant may bring destruction or victory. If the summit of the orator's art has been rightly defined to consist in knowing when to sit down, that of an advocate may be described as knowing when to keep his seat. Very little experience in our Courts will teach you this lesson, for every day will show to your observant eye instances of self-destruction brought about by imprudent cross-examination. Fear not that your discreet reserve may be mistaken for carelessness or want of self-reliance. The true motive will soon be seen and approved. Your critics are lawyers, who know well the value of discretion in an advocate, and how indiscretion in cross-examination cannot be compensated by any amount of ability in other duties. The attorneys are sure to discover the prudence that governs your tongue. Even if the wisdom of your absence be not apparent at the moment, it will be recognised in the result. Your fame may be of slower growth than that of the talker, but it will be larger and more enduring. The issue of a cause rarely depends upon a speech, and is but seldom even affected by it; but there is never a cause contested the result of which is not mainly dependent upon the skill with which the advocate conducts his cross-examination."

*   *   *   *   *

We have had frequent occasion to speak of Sir James Scarlett as an accomplished advocate, and we have endeavoured to learn from various writers the secret of his great success. While Scarlett did not often cross-examine at length, the following account of his method of conducting a cross-examination, we venture to say, will prove more instructive than many abstract precepts upon the subject. We trust that our readers will give it the most careful attention —

"In cross-examination he outstrips all that have ever appeared at the British Bar; not, perhaps, in one single quality—for while some have excelled him in strength and force, others have left him behind them in craft and wit. His superiority, however, as an accomplished

cross-examiner—as one combining the best qualities
for the office, and making the best use of them at the
best time and to the best effect—must on every hand
be admitted. His brow is never clothed with terror, and
his hand never aims to grasp the thunderbolt; but the
gentlemanly ease, the polished courtesy, and the
Christian urbanity and affection, with which he proceeds
to the task, do infinitely more mischief to the testimony of
witnesses who are striving to deceive, or upon whom he
finds it expedient to fasten a suspicion   He has often
thrown the most careful and cunning off their guard, by
the very behaviour from which they inferred their
security.   Seldom has he discouraged a witness by
harshness, and never by insult, and to put men upon
the defensive by a hostile attitude, he has always considered unwise and unsafe.   Hence he takes those he
has to examine, as it were, by the hand, makes them his
friends, enters into familiar conversation with them,
encourages them to tell him what will best answer his
purpose, and thus secures a victory without appearing
to commence a conflict."

The following remarks upon the subject of cross-
examination made by the learned Sir William David
Evans will be found instructive by the reader.—

" The cross-examination of witnesses adduced by the
opposite party is a subject of the utmost nicety, with
respect both to the conduct of the advocate, and the
discrimination of those who are to form a judgment;
and it is in this part of the cause that most of the
observations already suggested principally arise.   The
original examination of the witness (except in the case
of his giving an unwilling testimony), seldom gives much
room for observation; the statement is for the most part
sufficiently explicit and direct.   Sometimes that interest
which he may feel in the event will be apparent, and
thus assist the effect of the cross-examination; sometimes a real careless and indifference upon the subject

will produce an indolence of deportment; and a want
of exertion for the recollection of material occurrences
injurious to the party adducing him, in the same
manner as it has the effect of preventing a full and adequate representation of his case; but wherever this occurs
there is very little ground to expect that his cross-
examination will lead to any conclusions unfavourable to
the veracity of his statement This indifference is not
unfrequently assumed; whenever that is the case, it
seldom fails to be detected and exposed in the course of
a judicious cross-examination. If there is no apprehension that a witness has any other disposition than to give
a plain and succinct declaration of the truth, nor any
wish in the advocate to convey a different impression,
but his cross-examination is merely for the purpose of
explanation, or for ascertaining further facts of which
he may be supposed to have a knowledge, it is not to
be materially distinguished from his examination in
chief. The peculiar character of cross-examination only
attaches when it is suspected that the witness is guilty
of perjury, or at least misrepresentation or suppression
of facts, or when it is wished to convey that impression
to the jury; and it is a matter of daily experience that
this purpose is effected by an able and judicious cross-
examination, in many cases where the purposes of
justice would be eluded upon any different mode of
inquiry. The abuses to which this procedure is liable
are the subject of very frequent complaint, but it would
be absolutely impossible, by any but general rules, to
apply a preventive to these abuses, without destroying
the liberty upon which the benefits above adverted to
essentially depend; and all that can be effected by the
interposition of the Court is a discouragement of any
virulence towards the witnesses which is not justified by
the nature of the cause, and a sedulous attention to
remove from the minds of the jury the impressions
which are rather to be imputed to the vehemence of the

advocate, than to the prevarication of the witness. Whatever can elicit the actual dispositions of the witness with respect to the event, whatever can detect the operation of a concerted plan of testimony or bring into light the incidental facts and circumstances that the witness may be supposed to have suppressed, in short, whatever may be expected fairly to promote the real manifestation of the merits of the cause, it will be the duty of the advocate to put forward. But where the object of the client is merely to gratify his passions by unmerited abuse, by embarrassing or intimidating witnesses, of whose veracity he has no real suspicion, or by conveying an impression of discredit which he does not actually feel, in all cases of this kind, there is an imperious duty upon the advocate, who, while the protector of private right, is also the minister of public justice, which requires them to be repelled. Considering the subject merely as a matter of discretion, the adoption of an unfair conduct in cross-examination has often an effect repugnant to the interests which it professes to promote. In the case of *Hunter* v. *Kehoe*, before the Court of King's Bench in Ireland, Mic 1794, Ridgeway, etc, 350, Lord CLONMELL observed that cross-examinations had gone to an unreasonable length, but he had in general permitted gentlemen to go as far as they pleased, because if there was an honest case on the other side it would do them no good. But however unfavourable an injudicious asperity of cross-examination may be to the advancement of a cause, it is for the most part congenial to the wishes of the party, and the neglect of it is regarded as an indifference to his interest and a dereliction of duty; while the practice of it is one of the surest harbingers of professional success

The benefits of cross-examination are sometimes defeated by the interposition of the Court, to require an explanation of the motive and object of the questions proposed, or to pronounce a judgment upon their immateriality; whereas experience frequently shows that it is only by an indirect, and apparently irrelevant, inquiry that a witness can be brought to divulge the truth which he prepared himself to conceal, the explanation of the motives and tendency of the question furnishes the witness with a caution that may wholly defeat the object of it, which might have been successfully attained if the gradual progress from immateriality to materiality was withheld from his observation. The importance of an inquiry may sometimes be strongly felt by an advocate, and upon very reasonable grounds, from his own instructions with respect to the bearing and circumstances of his cause, which the Judge, acting only upon the impressions of what has already been disclosed, cannot by any possibility anticipate. The full expositions of the motives can only be attained by a premature exposition of the case that is to be brought forward, and even when that can be done without prejudice to the party, the endeavour to satisfy the Court would have the common effect of an interruption in the regular cause of inquiry, and instead of assisting the accurate discussion of the question, would in all probability terminate in confused and desultory altercation.

CHAPTER IV.

RE-EXAMINATION OF WITNESSES

THE chief object of re-examination is to give the witness an opportunity to explain what he said on cross-examination   During the examination in chief counsel who is to conduct the cross-examination should take notes of the testimony and enter on his brief the matters about which he wishes to cross-examine the witness, and during the progress of the cross-examination, counsel who is to re-examine his witness should also take notes of any questions he may wish to ask   It may not be out of place to remark here that an advocate will find the practice of taking full notes of all that is said by the Court, by opposing counsel and by the witnesses, very advantageous for many reasons.   Many eminent counsel never depart from this rule.   Rufus Choate took copious notes of all that was said during the progress of a trial in which he was engaged, notwithstanding the fact that he found it more difficult to read than to write them.

The advocate should keep his eye fixed upon his witness while he is being cross-examined so that he may discover any desire he may show to give an explanation of an answer, or to add something that would modify its apparent meaning He should carefully note upon his brief the result of his observations , he should also note any answers that appear to be damaging   The advocate will learn by experience by what signs a witness will indicate a desire to explain what he has said on cross-examination.

It is absolutely necessary, in many cases, to give a witness an opportunity, after he has been cross-examined, to explain any statements which he may have inadvertently made while he was undergoing a severe cross-examination. And, as we have said, an advocate whose duty it is to re-examine a witness must be on the alert to note every point which requires an explanation.

If the advocate is skilful, he will not only reinstate the witness whom he has called in the confidence of the Court and jury, if it has been shaken by the cross-examination, but he will secure a repetition of the most important portions of the testimony of the witness, and thus imprint it more firmly on the mind of the jury.

As a rule, in re-examination counsel should only touch upon matters brought out on cross-examination, and he must use great discretion in asking for explanation of what the witness stated on cross-examination. He should, before doing this, be satisfied that the witness can explain, satisfactorily, the apparent contradictions in his testimony, for it would be more hurtful to call for an explanation, and obtain one that is injurious, than to pass over in silence the point not susceptible of explanation.

After a witness has emerged from the fiery furnace of cross-examination, if we may use the expression, the probability is that he has been scorched, and that he is not in a very happy frame of mind, and the total or partial destruction of the testimony of his witness is not calculated to improve the good humour of counsel himself; therefore he must guard against showing the slightest sign of being disconcerted or dumbfounded at the ravages made in his case by that most dangerous and destructive engine, cross-examination, but he must proceed with the greatest coolness and patience to repair the damage which has been done him. Before beginning his re-examination, counsel should determine, in his own mind, what fact brought out in examination in chief has been displaced, or obscured, and what new matter has been introduced in answer to the questions of his opponent. Having in this manner taken a survey of the situation, he should, as nearly as possible, begin to repair the damage in the order in which it was done. We take

it for granted that the counsel has paid the strictest
attention to the cross-examination, and that he is, therefore, able to proceed in the work of repair as the destroyer
proceeded in his work of destruction.

Sir Frank Lockwood, on the occasion referred to on
page 36, said of re-examination —

"Re-examination—the putting Humpty-Dumpty together again—was by no means an unimportant portion
of an advocate's duty. Once, in the Court of Chancery,
a witness was asked in cross-examination by an eminent
Chancery leader, whether it was true that he had been
convicted of perjury. The witness owned the soft impeachment, and the cross-examining counsel very properly
sat down. Then it became the duty of an equally eminent
Chancery Q.C. to re-examine 'Yes,' said he, 'it is true
you have been convicted of perjury. But tell me Have
you not on many other occasions been accused of perjury, and been acquitted?' He recommended that as an
example of the way in which it ought not to be done."

If the testimony of your witness has not been shaken
upon cross-examination, and there is nothing that should
be explained, or nothing forgotten in your examination
in chief, dismiss the witness. Avoid re-examining as to
trifling matters ; besides taking up the time of the Court
and jury unnecessarily, the jurors may give undue
weight to things of no importance which you dwell upon
at length.

If an answer favourable to your side has been brought
out on cross-examination, don't press the witness to re-
state, you can comment upon it when you argue your
case to the jury

If your witness has been completely broken down upon
cross-examination, and has involved himself in hopeless
contradictions, hope nothing from him, but get rid of
him as soon as possible If, however, there is a chance
to set him on his feet, do it. If he has given an account
of a transaction susceptible of more than one construction,

aid him in giving the real character of the transaction, by asking suitable questions If his credibility has been assailed, re-establish it if possible, for the whole of his testimony rests upon that foundation The chances are that if questions have been asked a witness which have a tendency to impeach his credit he will be anxious to explain, and the jury will be apt to sympathise with him, and to feel relieved when he has given a satisfactory explanation of some transaction involving moral turpitude with which counsel cross-examining him sought to connect him.   It is dangerous to cross-examine as to character, as we have indicated in our chapter on that subject, unless the advocate asking the questions has good ground for making his attack upon the witness.

An instance where a witness was cross-examined as to character by a stupid advocate is given by Mr Richard Harris, K C, in his work upon advocacy, as follows: " I will give one instance out of many where character was once in my hearing cruelly assailed in cross-examination by an inexperienced advocate, and upon whom it recoiled with crushing severity.   He asked a witness if he had not been convicted of felony.   In vain the unfortunate victim in the box protested that it had nothing to do with the case. ' Have you not been convicted of felony ? ' persisted the counsel. ' Must I answer, my lord ? ' ' I am afraid you must,' answered his lordship. ' There is no help.   It will be better to answer it, as your refusal in any event would be as bad as the answer.' ' I have,' murmured the witness, under a sense of shame and confusion I never saw more painfully manifest. The triumphant counsel sat down.   Not long, however, was his satisfaction.

" In re-examination the witness was asked : ' When was it ? '

" A.—' Twenty-nine years ago.'

" The Judge —' You were only a boy ? '—Witness : ' Yes, my lord.'

"It need scarcely be added that a just and manly indignation burst from all parts of the Court, and the comments of the learned Judge were anything but complimentary to the injudicious advocate."

Counsel should be careful not to let in new matter upon re-examination and thus afford the opposing counsel the opportunity to re-cross-examine. While upon re-examination the advocate has not the right to ask questions upon matter which has not been brought out on the examination in chief, or cross-examination, without the permission of the Court being first asked and obtained, it may be that opposing counsel will not object to the introduction of the new matter, preferring to claim the right to re-cross-examine.

It is sometimes very unwise to object to a question where the answer is not very damaging, for the reason that the jury will suspect that some fact has been withheld which the party objecting wished to keep back, and they will always exaggerate its importance Jurors love to have all the light turned on, and they are apt to suspect that the litigant who wishes to hide behind a technical objection, especially if he does it often, is unworthy of their verdict.

Counsel should not have such an itch to re-examine as to disturb the case he has already made. His preparation of the case should always be so thorough as to leave nothing unproved by his direct examination, and, as we have said, he should carefully abstain from asking questions upon comparatively unimportant matters. He should let well enough alone. We have known many advocates get into deep water by not doing this. After proving their case clearly, they were not satisfied with their performance, but were determined to kick their assailant after he had been knocked down. The foolish course of such advocates reminds us of that of the Italian whose experience was embodied in the epitaph upon his tombstone, which read as follows · "I was

well, I wanted to feel better; I took physic, and here
I am."

The counsel who is to re-examine should be so
entirely familiar with the testimony of the witnesses in
his case that he will be in no danger of leaving anything unexplained. The remarks of Mr. Reed upon
this point are worthy of insertion here   He says · "We
have said that one purpose of a cross-examination was to
avoid the garbling of the testimony that could always
be ingeniously done on the examination in chief.   And
the great reason of the re-examination is to prevent a
like garbling by the cross-examining counsel.   The
cross-examination can not only deeply probe the witness
as to his feelings, his bias, his means of knowledge, but
it can also elicit from him independent facts favourable
to the examiner.   And by reason of the right of the
counsel to confine the witness to answer the questions,
and to permit him to give nothing else, only a portion
of the truth may be so presented as to impart falsehood.
Thus a witness who has testified in examination in chief
to an occurrence, may be asked in cross-examination if
it were not night, and answering affirmatively, he may
stand somewhat discredited until the re-examination
draws out that there was a good light, by which he
could see clearly.   Again, to apply differently an
example already given, an item of indebtedness of the
plaintiff to the defendant, pleaded as a set-off, may be
proven by the witness testifying under cross-examination to an admission of such indebtedness by the
plaintiff; but the re-examination may relieve by making
the witness testify that the plaintiff at the time of the
admission asserted the debt to be a gaming one, or one
otherwise illegal."

When an advocate notices that opposing counsel is
hectoring or bullying his witness he should go to the
relief of the witness, and object to such unfair treatment.   There are unscrupulous advocates, who in the

course of examination, will assume something to have been proven which has not been. When this occurs, the advocate prejudiced by the misstatement should immediately correct his adversary, but he should do so without undue heat.

Many excellent lawyers make objections to testimony for the purpose of having an objection entered on the record when they are overruled, but for fear that their objections will be sustained, do not strongly urge them. They do this for the purpose of laying the foundation for a new trial in case they are defeated.* But if the opposing counsel is equally shrewd, he can prevent the success of this artifice very often by withdrawing the testimony to which objection has been made, and if the testimony is not very important he should do so   We must again insist that the advocate should be as courteous as possible to witnesses while examining them.   He should take into consideration the fact that witnesses are, usually, unaccustomed to Courts, and to making an appearance in public, and that it is natural for them to feel ill at ease   He should not lose patience with them if their answers are incompetent, irrelevant, or not responsive to the questions asked them.   Apart from the fact that any other course would be ungentle-manly and indecorous, it is impolitic.   The jurors being laymen, and belonging to the same classes, and pursuing the same avocations that the large majority of witnesses are engaged in, become prejudiced against counsel who treat them unfairly.

Advocates who consume too much time in the exami-nation of witnesses soon become unpopular with juries and the Courts.   The leading points should, of course, be brought out in examination of each witness, but regard must be had to the allegations in the pleadings and the issues to be decided by the jury, and anything

---

* The practice to which Mr. Hardwicke here alludes, is not, it is thought, one which is common in the English Courts.

which does not bear upon the issues involved should be carefully avoided. While all questions respecting the examination of witnesses rest largely in the discretion of the Court, as a general rule the re-examination of a witness will not be allowed to extend to any new matter unconnected with the cross-examination, and which could have been inquired into upon the examination in chief.

If counsel conducting the re-examination wishes to question the witness about new matter, he should in every instance request permission of the Court to examine as to such matter. But in the re-examination of a witness counsel examining will be allowed to ask a witness any questions necessary to explain matters elicited from him upon cross-examination. For instance, if a witness has been asked upon cross-examination, for the purpose of discrediting him, as to vindictive or malignant expressions used by him, with reference to a third person, and has admitted upon such cross-examination that he did use such expressions, he may be asked upon his re-examination to explain, fully, all the circumstances under which those expressions were used, or he will be allowed to state what the person had done to provoke them.

As we have elsewhere stated, the Judge has full power in all cases, civil or criminal, to recall witnesses for examination in any stage of the case before it is finally disposed of

When the case for the defendant is closed, it is a general rule that the evidence in reply must bear directly or indirectly upon the subject-matter of the defence, and no new matter not connected with the defence, and not tending to disprove it, ought to be introduced. This general rule has been laid down by the Courts for the purpose of saving time and of preventing confusion and embarrassment, but the rule will always be relaxed by the Judge when the due administration of justice, or the discovery of truth, which is the prime object of every examination, demands such relaxation.

Thus if, after the plaintiff has closed his case, the defendant should introduce new and different evidence of such a nature as to take the plaintiff by surprise, the Judge may give leave to the plaintiff, if necessary, to produce fresh evidence, by way of rebuttal *Bigsby* v. *Dickinson*, 4 Ch. D 24

CHAPTER V.

SOME ELEMENTARY RULES.

REFERENCE has been made more than once in these pages to the fact that questions as to the admissibility of evidence generally arise suddenly and have to be dealt with on the spur of the moment. For this reason the advocate—if he is to be well equipped—should carry in his head some of the more important rules of evidence in order that he may object successfully to his opponent's questions, should the occasion arise, and also in order that he may justify his own questions if wrongly objected to

The thorough mastery of such rules will also enable the advocate to put forward his evidence in the proper manner, and so to make objection unnecessary.

The rules which are set out below are, it need hardly be said, only rough rules. They are not meant to exclude the study of works like Best on Evidence, Stephen's Digest of the Law of Evidence, Archbold's Criminal Pleadings, and, in particular cases, Roscoe's Nisi Prius Evidence.

But it is hoped that the advocate who has studied the Principles of the Law of Evidence in works of authority, such as those enumerated, may find the subjoined list of rules useful to jog his memory.

1. **What a person has stated (not on oath) is** Hearsay in- **not evidence**—You may not therefore in admissible general ask A (in examination in chief*) what in examina- B said Nor may you in general ask B. him- tion in chief. self (if he is your witness*), what he said on a former occasion about the matters at issue.

---

* Although, strictly speaking, hearsay is irrelevant, whether in examination in chief or in cross-examination, the practice in cross-examination is

Exceptions.—Where B. is a party —

(*a*) What B said may be part of the **res gestæ**, *i.e*, it may have accompanied an act and explained it, and in that case, if the act is part of the transaction being inquired into, both the act and the statement accompanying it (if it be necessary to explain the act) may be given in evidence, even though the statement was not made in the presence of the other party *Hyde* v. *Palmer*, 3 B. & S. 657

N.B.—In such a case both B. who made the statement and A. who heard it may give evidence of it.

Similarly, although a statement does not accompany an act, it may of itself amount to an act, and in that case the ordinary rules as to relevancy apply, and the rules as to hearsay do not apply ; *e.g.*, if B say at an auction, " Those goods are mine," these words may amount to a claim, and may be proved as such whether by B who uttered or by A. who heard the words *Cf. Ford* v. *Elliot*, 4 Exch. 78 ; *cf*. also the complaints of women who have been ravished.

(*b*) **Admissions and confessions** are evidence against the persons who made them, provided that they have been properly obtained · *vide* Stephen's Digest of Law of Evidence, 7th ed., p 24. The same applies to admissions made by agents, which are evidence against principals, if the agents have been expressly or impliedly authorised to make them *Clifford* v. *Burton*, 1 Bing. 199.

N.B.—In criminal cases the circumstances under which a confession has been obtained are generally

to give a very wide licence, and to presume that if counsel cross examines as to hearsay, it is because he is within one of the exceptions—as he generally is. If he is not, he runs the risk of eliciting what is more likely to harm than to help his case.

scrutinised with care. *vide* Archbold, Criminal Pleadings, 23rd ed., pp 325-339.

(*c*) What one party said to or in the hearing of the other party to the suit may be given in evidence by either party and by other witnesses.

N.B.—Similarly, in criminal cases, what is said in the presence of the accused is evidence, even if it be the confession of his fellow-accused incriminating him · Archbold, p. 330, but *vide R.* v. *Norton,* 26 T. L. R. 550

(*d*) A witness, even though not a party, may be contradicted by calling evidence that the witness spoke or wrote a **Different Account** from that given in the trial. And this may be done by the witness's own side, provided in the opinion of the Judge the witness has proved hostile: *ante,* pp 31, 35, 39.

Other particular exceptions to the rule which excludes hearsay are as follows —

(i.) In **Questions of Pedigree,** *Statements of deceased persons* (*blood relations*) may be given in evidence; *vide* Stephen's Digest of the Law of Evidence, 7th ed., pp. 43, 44.

(ii) In questions of **Public and General Rights,** *e.g.,* Public Right of Way, *statements of deceased persons who had competent means of knowledge* may be given in evidence; *ibid.,* pp. 41, 42.

(iii.) In all kinds of proceedings the statements of **deceased** persons (not parties), if when made they were *against the interest of the maker,* may be given in evidence: Roscoe's Nisi Prius Evidence, 18th ed., p. 55.

(iv.) In all kinds of proceedings the statements of deceased persons *in the regular discharge of their business* (*e.g.,* entries by a disinterested person in the books of a firm) may be given in evidence.

(v.) Dying declarations and depositions are admissible as evidence in certain criminal cases, but do not really fall under the head of hearsay evidence, as they are statements on oath ; *vide* Archbold, 23rd ed., p. 373.

2. **You may not ask leading questions of or cross-** Leading **examine your own witnesses relative to** Questions **matters** which are at issue in the suit   A leading question is one which suggests to the witness the answer which you expect him to make (*vide ante*, pp. 28, 29, 34, 35).

> **Exception** —Where a witness, in the opinion of the Judge, proves hostile to the side which calls him, the Judge may give permission to counsel on that side to put leading questions to him and to cross-examine him (*vide ante*, pp 31, 35, 39, 54, 55)

3. **You may not call evidence that a witness** Discrediting **called by yourself is not worthy of** one's own **credence .** *Ewer* v. *Ambrose*, 3 B & C. 749 witness   Having put him forward to the Court as a witness to be believed, you may not, if he prove hostile, attack his general character for veracity.   But you may contradict his evidence on the matters at issue, and by leave of the Court cross-examine him as to previous statements, and if necessary contradict him by such statements (*vide ante*, pp 31, 35, 39)

4. **You may not ask your own witnesses for their** **opinion** Opinion
> **Exception.**—In matters of science, expert witnesses are permitted to give their opinions.

5. **You may not prove the contents of a written** **document by oral evidence.** Oral Evi- dence of   **N.B.**—This applies equally to examination Documents and to cross-examination

Exceptions—

(*a*) Where the original document has been lost or destroyed, secondary evidence may be given of its contents, *i.e.*, a copy or oral evidence. But the loss or destruction must first be proved (*cf. ante*, pp. 11, 12, 67).

(*b*) Where the original document is in the possession of the other party to the suit, and he fails to comply with a notice to produce it at the trial, secondary evidence may be given of its contents (*ante*, pp. 5, 6).

(*c*) The admissions of a party to the suit as to the contents of a written document are primary evidence of the contents of a document, and such admissions may either be elicited from the party who made them in cross-examination, or proved by the evidence of other witnesses. *Slatterie* v. *Pooley*, 6 M. & W 664; 55 R. R. 760.

Copies of Documents.

6 You may not prove the contents of a written document by means of a copy.*

Exceptions—

(*a*) Where oral evidence may be given (*see* rule 5, *ante*), the document may also be proved by a copy.

(*b*) Certain documents of a public character which may either by common law or statutes be proved by (1) exemplifications, (11) office copies, (111) examined copies, (1v.) certified copies. (As to the appropriateness of these various kinds of copies, *vide* Roscoe's Nisi Prius Evidence, pp. 96 *et seq.*)

(*c*) Under an order of the Master made in pursuance of R. S C, Order XXX., r. 7, which is as follows .—"On the hearing of the summons, the

* Counterparts of deeds are not copies, but are primary evidence against the parties who executed them

Court or a Judge may order that evidence of any particular fact, to be specified in the order, shall be given by statement on oath of information and belief, or by production of documents or entries in books, or by copies of documents or entries or otherwise, as the Court or Judge may direct."

As to the use of a copy of a memorandum for the purpose of refreshing the memory, *see* below, rule 9.

7. Where a **contract** has been reduced into writing, Oral Evi- it is presumed that all the terms o the dence of Written contract are included in the writing. You Contracts may not therefore by oral evidence add to, subtract from, or vary the writing.

(Further, by the Statute of Frauds and the Sale of Goods Act, s. 4, the contracts therein specified may not be sued upon unless in writing and signed by the party to be charged.)

Exceptions—

(*a*) Where it appears from the writing itself that the whole of the terms are not included in the contract, the presumption is rebutted, and oral evidence may therefore be admissible to show the complete contract. (N.B.—But this does not apply to the contracts required by the Statute of Frauds and the Sale of Goods Act to be in writing.)

(*b*) Latent' (as opposed to patent) ambiguities may be explained by oral evidence.

(*c*) You may call oral evidence to rebut the presumption referred to above, and to prove that the writing does not include the whole contract · *Elmore v. Kingscote* (1826), 5 B. & C. 583.

---

* Latent ambiguities are those which do not appear upon the face of the document, *e g*, "My nephew Charles," in a will, where the testator has in fact two nephews named Charles. Patent ambiguities are those which are clear on the face of the document, *e.g*, an obscurity in the language itself, or the grammar.

(d) You may call oral evidence to prove that the writing which purports to be a writing of the contract does not record any previous parol contract: *Pym* v. *Campbell*, 6 E. & B. 370, *i.e.*, that the parties were never *ad idem* or that the contract was subject to a condition, which was not fulfilled.

(e) You may call oral evidence of a parol agreement collateral to the written agreement, provided that the parol agreement does not modify or contradict any of the terms of the written agreement · *Erskine* v. *Adeane*, L. R. 8 Ch. 756, *De Lassalle* v. *Guildford*, [1901] 2 K. B. 215.

(f) You may call oral evidence to prove that a written contract was obtained by fraud, illegality, or that it contains an error.*

(g) You may, in general, prove failure of consideration, *e.g.*, in the case of bills, notes, etc., in spite of such words as " for value received " · *Ex parte Carter*, 12 Ch. D 908.

(h) If the written contract was one which need not have been in writing (*i.e.*, is not within the Statute of Frauds or the Sale of Goods Act) you may prove, by parol evidence, a subsequent waiver or discharge of some or all of the terms *Mercantile Bank of Sydney* v. *Taylor*, [1893] A. C. 317.

(i) You may, in general, prove usage and custom† which affect the meaning of words in a written contract, whether mercantile or agricultural, and to explain terms of art, provided they do not expressly

---

* If the error is one which goes to the root of the contract, it would seem that oral evidence can only be given of it in an action for rectification

† In this respect it is important to remember that in law a custom is one which is so universally acquiesced in that everyone likely to be affected by it may be presumed to have known it, and therefore not to have troubled to set it out expressly in the contract Usage need not be so universal, old, or well known as custom, but must be reasonable . *Plaire* v *Allcock* 4 F & F. 1074, *Re Goetz*, [1898] 1 Q B 787

contradict the writing . *Grant* v. *Maddox*, 15 M. & W. 737 , *Parker* v. *Ibbetson*, 4 C. B. (N S) 346

(*j*) Where the party has made private memorandum of an oral agreement, private memorandum does not exclude oral proof of the agreement.

8. You may not give evidence of what has been "Without said or written between the parties Prejudice" "without prejudice."
Exceptions—

(*a*) Where the negotiations "without prejudice" have terminated in an agreement

(*b*) Where the writing or statement "without prejudice" in fact tends to prejudice your client, and he has therefore elected not to treat the writing or statement as "without prejudice" *Ex parte Holt*, [1893] 2 Q B 116

9. A witness may refresh his memory by referring Refreshing to a memorandum of the facts, provided Memory by it was made by himself at or soon after Memoranda the time of the occurrence : *Kensington* v. *Inglis*, 8 East, 289

If the witness's memory has been so refreshed that— having read it—he can swear positively to the facts, it makes no difference that the memorandum which he uses in Court is not the original but merely a copy or an extract , though it may well be matter for comment. If on the other hand the memorandum does not enable the witness to swear positively as to the facts, his evidence would merely amount to this, that he has or had a memorandum, which he made at the time, of facts which he cannot now remember; and the best and only admissible evidence of the contents of such a memorandum is the memorandum itself *Doe d. Church* v. *Perkins*, 3 T R 749; *Beech* v *Jones*, 5 C. B 696. If the memorandum, though made by someone else, was inspected soon after by the witness (*e.g.*, a log-book, properly kept and inspected by the captain), the witness may refresh his memory with it, provided it enables him to swear to the actual facts. *Burrough* v. *Martin*, 2 Camp. 112.

10. **You may not ask witnesses, whom you have called, to the character of a party or a** Evidence of Character **prisoner, (a) concerning particular acts of the party or prisoner which point to good character, nor may you ask a witness (b) his opinion of the party or prisoner.**

Questions of the nature of (a) are irrelevant, and questions of the nature of (b) transgress Rule 4.

The proper form of such a question is :—

"What reputation or character does A. B. bear?" (*ibid*, *R.* v. *Rowton*, L. & C. 520 ; *R.* v. *Jones*, 31 St. Trials, 310),

or if the witness be called for or against the credibility of a witness or party, the proper form of such a question is :—

"Is the witness a man who, from his general reputation, is to be believed on his oath?" (*ibid.*, *R.* v. *Brown*, L. R. 1 C. C. R. 70)

11. **Where a cause or matter is tried by a Judge with a jury, no communication to the jury** Payment into Court **shall be made until after the verdict is given, either of the fact that money has been paid into Court, or of the amount paid in.** The jury shall be required to find the amount of the debt or damages, as the case may be, without reference to any payment into Court.

The above is in the words of R. S. C., Order XXII, r. 22, and applies even to those cases where liability is admitted, and where consequently the only real issue is whether the defendant's payment is sufficient or not: *Jaques v. South Essex Waterworks Co.*, 20 T. L. R. 563. You must therefore avoid putting to the witnesses any question which would tend to elicit this information.

12. You may not, as counsel for the Crown, ask a prisoner who is giving evidence in his own behalf, or any other witness, any que tending to show that the prisoner * (a) has been committed, convicted, or charged with any offence other than that wherewith he is then charged; or (b) that he is of bad character.

Previous Convictions of Prisoners.

Exceptions.—(i) Where the proof of such convictions, etc., is admissible evidence upon the charge then made, *e g*, where several offences form one entire transaction, evidence may be given of all upon an indictment for one; or where it is necessary to prove a design, system, criminal intention, or guilty knowledge, as in charges for uttering counterfeit coin, receiving stolen goods, etc , *vide* Archbold's Criminal Pleadings, 23rd ed., pp. 307 *et seq.*

(ii) Where the prisoner endeavours by his questions or by his evidence to establish his own good character, or to make imputations on the character of the prosecutor or the witnesses for the prosecution.

(iii.) Where he has given evidence against any other person charged with the same offence.

N.B.—The reason of this rule is that in criminal cases, other than those referred to in the exceptions, the bad character of the prisoner is immaterial: *Makin v Attorney-General for N S.W.*, [1894] A. C. 57; 63 L. J. (P.C.) 41, and *vide* Criminal Evidence Act, 1898, s. 1 (*f*)

* This rule does not prevent you asking witnesses (other than the prisoner himself) whether they (the witnesses) have been convicted; *vide ante*, p 23, note

APPENDIX.

FORMS.

1. Affidavit as to Documents (O 31, r 13).

19   [*Here put letter and number*]

In the High Court of Justice.
Division
Between A B ,   Plaintiff,
and
C D ,   Defendant.

I, the above named defendant C D , make oath and say as follows —

1 I have in my possession or power the documents relating to the matters in question in this suit set forth in the first and second parts of the first schedule hereto

2 I object to produce the said documents set forth in the second part of the said first schedule hereto [*state grounds of objection*]

3 I have had, but have not now, in my possession or power the documents relating to the matters in question in this suit set forth in the second schedule hereto

4 The last-mentioned documents were last in my possession or power on [*state when, and what has become of them, and in whose possession they now are*]

5 According to the best of my knowledge, information, and belief I have not now, and never had in my possession, custody, or power, or in the possession, custody, or power of my solicitors or agents, solicitor or agent, or in the possession, custody, or power of any other persons or person on my behalf, any deed, account, book of account, voucher, receipt, letter, memorandum, paper, or writing, or any copy of or extract from any such document, or any other document whatsoever, relating to the matters in question in this suit, or any of them, or wherein any entry has been made relative to such matters, or any of them, other than and except the documents set forth in the said first and second schedules hereto

[NOTE —This form has been altered to accord with the official form now in use.]

---

2   Notice to Produce Documents (O 31, 1 16)

[*Heading as in Form 1*]

Take notice that the [*plaintiff or defendant*] requires you to produce for his inspection the following documents referred to in your [*statement of claim, or defence, or affidavit, dated the   day of   19   ]

Describe documents required

X Y , Solicitor to the

To Z , Solicitor for   .

3 Notice to Inspect Documents (O 31, r. 17).

[Heading as in Form 1]

Take notice that you can inspect the documents mentioned in your notice of the   day of   19   *[except the deed numbered in that notice]* at *[insert place of inspection]* on Thursday next the   instant between the hours of 12 and 4 o'clock

Or, that the *[plaintiff or defendant]* objects to giving you inspection of the documents mentioned in your notice of the   day of 19   , on the ground that *[state the ground]* :—

---

4. Notice to Produce (general form) (O. 32, r. 8).

[Heading as in Form 1]

Take notice, that you are hereby required to produce and show to the Court on the trial of this   all books, papers, letters, copies of letters, and other writings and documents in your custody, possession, or power, containing any entry, memorandum, or minute relating to the matters in question in this   , and particularly

Dated the   day of   , 19 .
To the above-named

h   solicitor *or* agent   .

(Signed)   , of
agent for   , solicitor
for the above-named

---

5. Notice to Admit Documents (O 32, r 3)

[Heading as in Form. ']

Take notice that the plaintiff *[or* defendant] in this cause proposes to adduce in evidence the several documents hereunder specified, and that the same may be inspected by the defendant *[or* plaintiff], his solicitor or agent, at   , on   , between the hours of   , and the defendant *[or* plaintiff] is hereby required, within forty-eight hours from the last-mentioned hour, to admit that such of the said documents as are specified to be originals were respectively written, signed, or executed, as they purport respectively to have been, that such as are specified as copies are true copies   and such documents as are stated to have been served, sent, or delivered, were so served, sent, or delivered respectively , saving all just exceptions to the admissibility of all such documents as evidence in this cause

Dated, &c   (Signed)
G H , solicitor *[or* agent] for plaintiff *[or* defendant]
To E F , solicitor *[or* agent] for defendant *[or* plaintiff]
[Here describe the documents, the manner of doing which may be as follows —]

6 Notice to Admit Facts (O. 32, r. 5).

[Heading as in Form 1.]

Take notice that the plaintiff [*or* defendant] in this cause requires the defendant [*or* plaintiff] to admit, for the purposes of this cause only, the several facts respectively hereunder specified ; and the defendant [*or* plaintiff] is hereby required, within six days from the service of this notice, to admit the said several facts, saving all just exceptions to the admissibility of such facts as evidence in this cause

Dated, &c

G. D., solicitor [*or* agent] for the plaintiff [*or* defendant].

To E F., solicitor [*or* agent] for the defendant [*or* plaintiff].

The facts, the admission of which is required, are—

1. That John Smith died on the 1st of January, 1890.
2. That he died intestate
3 That James Smith was his only lawful son
4 That Julius Smith died on the 1st of April, 1896.
5. That Julius Smith never was married

---

7. Interrogatories (O. 31, r. 4).

19 . *[Here put letter and number]*

In the High Court of Justice,
Division

Between A B , Plaintiff,

and

C D , E F , and G.H., Defendants.

Interrogatories on behalf of the above-named [*plaintiff*, *or* *defendant C D.*] for the examination of the above-named [*defendants E F.* and *G H.*, *or* *plaintiff*].

1. Did not, &c.
2. Has not, &c

&c. &c &c

[The defendant E.F is required to answer the interrogatories numbered .]

[The defendant G H. is required to answer the interrogatories numbered]

INDEX.

BRADBURY, AGNEW, & CO. LD. LONDON AND TONBRIDGE

Lightning Source UK Ltd.
Milton Keynes UK
UKOW05f1825270717

306195UK00015B/331/P